CHURCHILL'S FLAWED DECISIONS

ERRORS IN OFFICE OF THE GREATEST BRITON

CHURCHILL'S FLAWED DECISIONS

ERRORS IN OFFICE OF THE GREATEST BRITON

Stephen Wynn

PEN & SWORD
HISTORY

AN IMPRINT OF PEN & SWORD BOOKS LTD.
YORKSHIRE - PHILADELPHIA

First published in Great Britain in 2020 by
Pen & Sword Military
An imprint of
Pen & Sword Books Limited
Yorkshire - Philadelphia

Copyright © Stephen Wynn, 2020

ISBN 978 1 52670 8 540

Printed and bound in the UK by TJ International, Padstow, Cornwall

Pen & Sword Books Limited incorporates the imprints of Atlas,
Archaeology, Aviation, Discovery, Family History, Fiction, History,
Maritime, Military, Military Classics, Politics, Select, Transport,
True Crime, Air World, Frontline Publishing, Leo Cooper, Remember
When, Seaforth Publishing, The Praetorian Press, Wharncliffe Local
History, Wharncliffe Transport, Wharncliffe True Crime and White Owl.

For a complete list of Pen & Sword titles please contact

PEN & SWORD BOOKS LIMITED
47 Church Street, Barnsley, South Yorkshire S70 2AS, United Kingdom
E-mail: enquiries@pen-and-sword.co.uk
Website: www.pen-and-sword.co.uk

or

PEN AND SWORD BOOKS
1950 Lawrence Rd, Havertown, PA 19083, USA
E-mail: Uspen-and-sword@casematepublishers.com
Website: www.penandswordbooks.com

Contents

Introduction

It doesn't get any better than this, having the opportunity to write a book about the late, great, Winston Churchill. It will be slightly different to most books written about the great man as it will look at the errors he made whilst in office, either as an MP, in a political or military sense or as the prime minister of the UK. Despite the title, this book is in no way intended to try and besmirch his character or good name, but to look at some of the difficult decisions he had to make across his lifetime, especially the ones that didn't work out quite as intended. The book will also look at the young Winston growing up, his personality, his military career, and his life in politics, which is the arena he was in when he had to make the decisions, and which with the benefit of hindsight, were not all the best ones he ever made. Where possible I will look at why those decisions were made.

His decisions which I feel require further examination are the Sidney Street Siege in London in January 1910; the Dardanelles campaign (also referred to as Gallipoli) of 1915 and 1916, during the First World War, which resulted in some 120,000 British casualties and his subsequent decision to resign and return to a life in the military; the collapse of Singapore to the Japanese in February 1942; the sinking of the SS *Lancastria* in 1942 and the subsequent cover-up and the Bengal famine of 1943 when an estimated 3 million Indians died. I will take a look at his life between the wars and from when he became prime minister in 1940 through until May 1945, the Malayan emergency that took place between 1948 and 1960, and the Mau Mau Uprising in British Kenya, between 1952 and 1964.

Chapter 1

Churchill's Younger Years

To try and understand what might be classed as some of Churchill's stranger decisions, I thought it would useful to find out more about him as a person. To achieve that, I am going to take a look at his younger years, and his upbringing, to see if there were any obvious warning signs of what was to follow. I believe that just learning a bit about him as a man in general, is also useful.

Winston Leonard Spencer-Churchill was born on 24 January 1874, at his family's ancestral home of Blenheim Palace in Oxfordshire, to a wealthy aristocratic family.

His father, Lord Randolph Churchill, had been the Conservative MP for Woodstock since 1873, and his mother, Jenny Churchill, was American from an extremely wealthy family, who had built their fortune in finance. Randolph and Jenny's had been somewhat of a whirlwind romance. They had first met in August 1873, and after just three days had become engaged, and just eight months later, in April 1874, they were married at the British Embassy in Paris.

At the time of Churchill's birth, the United Kingdom was the most dominant nation in the world, and he was born into one of the country's most elite families. His grandfather on his father's side was John Spencer-Churchill, the 7th Duke of Marlborough, and a Conservative MP who served in the government of Benjamin Disraeli.

When Winston Churchill was just 2 years old, his grandfather, John Spencer-Churchill, was appointed as the Viceroy of Ireland, at a time when Ireland was undivided and part of the United Kingdom. Keeping things in the family, the new viceroy appointed his son, Randolph Churchill, as his private secretary, and so it was that the entire Churchill family, including 2-year-old Winston, upped and moved to Ireland.

It was a strange time for a young Winston as in the absence for long periods of time of his mother, Jenny, he spent much of the 1880s being brought up by a nanny, Elizabeth Everest, of whom Churchill became extremely fond. As for his relationship with his father Randolph, there wasn't much of one at all. During their time in Ireland, Churchill and his younger brother, Jack, were privately educated by a governess, which meant much of their younger formative years were quite isolated ones, in that they didn't have a massive circle of friends.

Theirs would have been somewhat of a closeted world where other than their governess, nanny and servants, they would have had very little contact with the outside world or anybody other than people from their own level of society. Young Winston would have lived a life of luxury, where he lived an opulent lifestyle, whether that was accommodation, clothes or food, leaving him with little or no understanding of the real value of money.

In 1883, when young Winston was just 7, the family moved back to London, and set up home at 2 Connaught Place, Bayswater, in the City of Westminster. It would remain the family home until 1892. But despite his tender years, Winston became a boarder at St George's School, Ascot in Berkshire, and only returned home during the school holidays. It was not a good time of his life and not an experience that he particularly enjoyed. Academically, he did not excel, and was often in trouble with his masters because of his bad behaviour. In fairness to Churchill, it must have felt somewhat strange as a 7-year-old boy not living in the bosom of his family, or being loved and cared for by his parents on a daily basis. At a time of their lives when most children were being read a bedtime story and tucked up in bed by their mother, Churchill was sleeping in a dormitory with a number of other boys, devoid of any love or affection, most probably crying himself to sleep most nights, wondering what he had done wrong to warrant such a life. Maybe his bad behaviour was connected to his emotional state of mind, and the feelings of being unloved and unwanted that ran around inside his head.

When he was 10 years old he continued his education at the Brunswick School in Hove, an independent school for boys aged between 3 and 13. The main reason for this move was because of its location closer to the coast, which was deemed to be better for his ailing health. There were pros and cons to his move of school. The downside was that his behaviour didn't greatly improve, although his academic work did.

At 14 years old he passed the entrance exams for the prestigious school at Harrow, where he continued his overall academic improvement. Even at that age he was a natural when it came to written prose, which in part provided him with an enjoyment and a gift for writing poetry.

Even though his relationship with his father hadn't been a particularly close one, it was he who determined that his son should be prepared for a future military life. Whether that was how Churchill saw his own life and career mapped out is unclear, but that was the normality for many young men of a certain social class back then. What a boy was going to do or be in life was decided by his parents, or at least his father.

In September 1893, his education continued at the Royal Military Academy, Sandhurst, when at the third attempt he passed the entrance exam, and was accepted as a cadet in the cavalry. What followed was fifteen months of military education that would provide a young cadet with the skills, knowledge and ability to become a credible officer and a leader of other men. He graduated from Sandhurst in January 1895, shortly before his father died.

Having graduated, Churchill found himself being commissioned as a second lieutenant in the 4th Queens Own Hussars, which had been a regiment in the British Army since 1685, and was first raised by the Hon. John Berkeley to help deal with the Monmouth Rebellion. The regiment's name at that time was The Princess Anne of Denmark's Regiment of Dragoons.

Churchill was keen to experience military action at first hand, which was after all what he was ultimately training for. To achieve this he used the influence of his mother who, through well-placed friends in America, managed to make Churchill's wish come true. In around October 1895 he travelled to Cuba to 'observe' its War of Independence. He was accompanied on his travels by friend and fellow officer with the 4th Queens Own Hussars, Reginald Barnes. Together they joined Spanish troops fighting against Cuban independence fighters, and became involved in numerous skirmishes.

Both Barnes and Churchill were in Cuba with the knowledge and approval of the British authorities, and under the command of the Director of British Military Intelligence, Colonel Edward Chapman.

Barnes was there in the capacity of an observer of guerrilla warfare to the Spanish army, whilst Churchill had been accredited as a journalist with the *London Daily Graphic* newspaper to send despatches about the war. Their real tasks were to collect information and statistics on various matters they were witness to, in particular the effect of a new bullet that was being used, how far it penetrated a man's body, and its striking power.

This was Churchill's first exposure to war and all the horrors that went with it. Seeing a man die in battle would have also been a new experience for him.

Reginald Barnes went on to serve in both the Second Boer War, where he was Mentioned in Despatches and awarded the Distinguished Service Order, as well as the First World War, where he was awarded the French Croix de Guerre. Sir Reginald Walter Ralph Barnes retired from the army in March 1921, having reached the rank of major general.

Churchill and Barnes returned to England after their informative reconnaissance in Cuba, but they were not home that long when they were off again, this time with the 4th Queens Own Hussars. They arrived in Bombay, India, in October 1896, and soon after were transferred to Bangalore, where Churchill and Barnes shared a bungalow for their accommodation.

Churchill spent some nineteen months stationed in India, during which he spent time in Calcutta, Hyderabad, as well as the North-West Frontier. This was his first experience of India, its people and its culture, and despite its appealing climate and beautiful views, the best Churchill could come up with by way of a description was 'a Godless land of snobs and bores'. Coming as he did from the privileged level of aristocratic society, how he used the word 'snob' without bursting into laughter, I am not sure.

At the same time, Churchill appeared to have had an epiphany about the extent of his level of education. Despite having attended both Harrow and the Royal Military College at Sandhurst, he thought of himself as being poorly educated. To address this, he set about reading numerous different works by some of the world's greatest thinkers, historians, and theologians from across the years, including Plato and Charles Darwin.

On 26 July 1897, the British garrison at Malakand came under attack by Pashtun rebels. The troops at the garrison managed to hold out for six days before a relief column including the Malakand Field Force, managed to lift the siege.

Churchill asked General Sir Bindon Blood if he could join the Malakand Field Force of which Blood was the commander, and who were engaged in a fight against the Mohmand rebels in the Swat Valley region of north-west India. Blood agreed to Churchill's request but only on the proviso he was there purely as a journalist. To meet this requirement, accreditation was acquired from the *Daily Telegraph* as well as the *Pioneer*.

In his writings home he detailed how both sides in the conflict showed no respect to their enemies. Any wounded who were captured were systematically slaughtered without a second thought, although no mention was made in Churchill's despatches of British troops having carried any out such acts. The Malakand Field Force consisted of one British cavalry regiment, one Indian cavalry regiment and one Indian infantry battalion. Churchill remained with the British troops for six weeks, and then returned to Bangalore in October 1897, where he wrote his first book, *The Story of the Malakand Field Force*.

Still in Bangalore and looking for a new challenge, Churchill got wind of General Sir Herbert Kitchener's planned military campaign in the Sudan. The latter didn't really have much time for Churchill, seeing him as a self-promoting individual who was simply seeking fame and publicity. Not to be put off by Kitchener's negativity towards him, Churchill returned to England and sought out none other than British Prime Minister, Lord Salisbury. With such powerful and influential friends to call upon, it was no great shock that Churchill got his own way, agreeing to write a column for the *Morning Post* newspaper.

He travelled by sea to Egypt, and on reaching Cairo, he joined up with the 21st Lancers and headed south along the River Nile, where they were to confront the Sudanese leader, Abdallah ibn Muhammad and his army at the Battle of Omdurman, which took place on 2 September 1898.

It was afterwards that Churchill showed his different sides, which to an extent highlighted some of his complexities. He wasn't afraid to stand up for himself and say what he felt needed saying. To start with he was highly critical of what he saw as Kitchener's more than ungentlemanly behaviour towards the Sudanese wounded, not at all what Churchill expected of a fellow officer, especially one as high ranking as Kitchener. He was also critical of Kitchener's conduct in the desecration of Muhammad Ahmad's tomb at Omdurman. If Kitchener was slightly perturbed by Churchill's direct opinion of how he conducted himself towards enemy prisoners, he wouldn't have been any happier when he discovered that Churchill had included his views in a book he had written about the campaign entitled *The River War*, which was first published in November 1899.

By the time of the book's second edition, published in 1902, his earlier criticism of Kitchener had been watered down somewhat. Maybe this was to do with not wanting to be seen by the British public as someone who was bad-mouthing a real life hero, as Kitchener was perceived to be back home. As he had become more politically savvy, he knew that it would serve no purpose in alienating himself in their eyes.

Besides writing, Churchill had also developed a strong enough interest in politics to orchestrate his way into being selected as the prospective Conservative MP for Oldham in Lancashire in the June 1899 by-election, but the seat was won by the Liberals.

The Second Boer War proved to be an interesting time for Churchill. Sensing that Britain and the Boer republics would soon be going to war against each other, he acquired war correspondent credentials from both the *Daily Mail* and the *Morning Post* newspaper organisations and made his way to South Africa, having sailed from Southampton. He arrived in Cape Town in October 1899, before travelling to where fighting was taking place near Ladysmith, which at the time was being besieged by Boer troops.

Whilst travelling to Natal, the train he was on was derailed by an artillery shell, and he was captured by the Boers and interned in one of their PoW camps in Pretoria. But Churchill had no intention of spending the rest of the war incarcerated in a Boer PoW camp, so along with two other inmates, he managed to make good his escape in December 1899. After stowing away on two freight trains and being helped out by an English mine owner, he managed to escape to Portuguese East Africa, and from there he caught a boat to Durban. Unbeknown to Churchill, his exploits were being followed by the British public who were suitably impressed with his acts of derring-do.

But rather than returning home to England as some might have expected him to, he stayed in South Africa and became a lieutenant in the South African Light Horse Regiment, and was involved in the fighting to relieve the Siege of Ladysmith and the taking of Pretoria. All the while he was still sending back despatches for the *Morning Post* newspaper, which included his hopes that the Boers would be treated with 'generosity and tolerance' and the fact that he didn't understand the British hatred for the Boer.

Churchill arrived back in England in July 1900 and rented a flat in an affluent area of Mayfair, in West London, which remained his home for a few years.

Not put off by his Oldham by-election loss the previous year, he once again stood as the Conservative candidate for Oldham in the 1900 general election, which took place between 25 September and 24 October. At that time the town elected two MPs, one of whom was Winston Churchill, the other the Liberal candidate, Alfred Emmott. An interesting statistic about that year's general election, was that there were four candidates, two Conservative and two Liberal. There were only 425 votes separating all four candidates with each of them receiving 12,500 votes and above. Winston Churchill was now a MP at just 25 years old, but there was a slight problem. In 1900, MPs were not paid a wage, unless they were a member of the Cabinet, so to earn himself some much-needed money, he arranged a speaking tour which saw him visiting towns and cities across England, Europe, America and Canada. The talks he gave focused on his experiences in South Africa, and in October 1900, he had a book published on the same subject entitled *Ian Hamilton's March*.

Between 1899 and 1900, Churchill earned himself a staggering sum of £10,000 (approximately £1.2m in today's money – 2019) from his speaking tour, books, journals and newspaper columns he had written.

Although Churchill had an interesting and varied life up until the age of 25, his social standing and place in society helped him greatly. There are not too many people who could just up and sail to South Africa, stay at the viceroy's premises in India, visit the prime minister at 10 Downing Street, obtain Press accreditation, or rent a flat in Mayfair, then decide they wanted to become an MP, or have a book published. So I think it is fair to say that Churchill certainly had what could be classed as a privileged upbringing, and partly due to that, I believe it also gave him a somewhat distorted view of life. He had experienced war at first hand, and had travelled far and wide, where he saw for himself the squalor that some people lived in and their daily struggle for survival, with little or no food, but he had never personally gone without food, nor been able to put a roof over his head.

The question is, did any of these experiences affect his decision-making process in later years, especially when he was in a position of power and control?

Chapter 2

Early Political Issues

By 1904, Churchill no longer agreed with Conservative values and politics, instead preferring those of the Liberal Party, who he then 'crossed the floor' to join. Opinion was split in the corridors of Parliament as to why Churchill had changed sides. There were those who believed it was because of his desire to eliminate poverty and his concerns for working class people, whilst the more cynical believed his decision was for no other reason than a desire for a ministerial post which would bring with it a wage.

Henry Campbell-Bannerman, later Sir Henry Campbell-Bannerman, had been the leader of the Liberal Party from 1899. Between 1895 and December 1905, the country had been led by a Conservative and Liberal Unionist coalition, but on 5 December 1905, the Conservative Prime Minister, Arthur Balfour, resigned, in part due to continuing political unpopularity, some of which was due to the poor social state of the country, which was highlighted as a result of the Boer War. It is estimated that more than 40 per cent of military recruits who looked to enlist were rejected due to being unfit for military service, a direct correlation to the poverty of the nation, where it was estimated that a third of the country's people lived below what was classed as the 'poverty line'.

Balfour's resignation led to the 1906 general election which took place between 12 January and 8 February, and led to Campbell-Bannerman becoming the new prime minister after a landslide Liberal victory, a position he held until 1908. The 1906 election was the last time the Liberal Party won a general election outright, but Churchill didn't contest his seat for Oldham which he won as a Conservative, instead he won the carefully selected Manchester North-West seat, which had been a Conservative-held seat since it was created in 1885.

Under Campbell-Bannerman, Churchill was given the position of Under-Secretary of State for the Colonies.

In early 1906, Churchill gave his first speech in the House, but it didn't go particularly well for him. He spoke about the adoption of 'constitutions for the defeated Boer republics of the Transvaal and the Orange River Colony', and about the use of 'Chinese slave labour' in South African mines. In his speech, Churchill tried to defend Lord Miller, an influential figure in the Liberal Party in the role of formulating foreign and domestic policy, whilst at the same time distancing himself from his policies. That was always going to be a hard 'trick' to pull off, even for Churchill, and consequently he totally misread the mood of the House. What was particularly frustrating from Churchill's point of view was that he had written the speech himself, and had even rehearsed his delivery in front of a member of his own staff. My assumption, based on the fact that Churchill went ahead with the speech, is that the member of staff told him that he was happy with it. Whether he was being truthful, or just told him what he thought he wanted to hear, is not known. The fact that Churchill did not see the potential downfall of his own speech is the real surprise. It is one thing for a person to speak their mind and stick to their principles, based on what they think is right, but they must also have a grasp of their audience's views, and have a feel for how they will receive what is going to be said.

The reality of the situation is that he got it wrong, and his first speech as Under-Secretary of State for the Colonies, although not bad enough to end his ministerial role, was not an auspicious beginning for him.

Despite him not being a Cabinet minister, and still only an under-secretary, Campbell-Bannerman had put forward Churchill for promotion to the Cabinet, as by then he had become a prominent member of the government, but the king, Edward VII, took the somewhat surprising decision of vetoing Churchill from being appointed to the Cabinet.

On 3 April 1908, Herbert H. Asquith, who had been the Chancellor of the Exchequer up to that point in time, became prime minister when Campbell-Bannerman had resigned due to ill health, the result of a number of heart attacks. Not wanting to die in office and risk the possibility of a general election, he resigned. His decision proved to be right, borne out by the fact that he died on 2 April 1908, just three weeks after his resignation.

One of the first decisions Asquith took was to promote Churchill to the Cabinet as the President of the Board of Trade, making him the youngest member of the Cabinet since the mid-1850s.

Asquith had a daughter, Violet Asquith, who in 1908, was 21. She was particularly smitten with a single man who at 33, was twelve years older than her. The man in question was Winston Churchill. They had first met in April 1907, and got on well with each other, having a few similar traits in common: both were strong willed, idealistic and highly opinionated, to name but a few. They were not engaged but spent a lot of time together. Arrangements between the couple were made for Churchill to go and stay with Violet and her family on 17 August 1908 at Slains Castle at Cruden Bay on the Scottish coast, which the family had rented. Maybe this was to be the start of something serious.

When Violet's father became prime minister in April 1908 she told him to, 'Make the most of Winston', to which he is said to have replied, 'You need have no fear on Winston's account. He will be well looked after and provided for.'

In the meantime, and unbeknown to Violet, Churchill was somewhat smitten with the granddaughter of the Earl of Airlie, 22-year-old, Clementine Hozier, who he had invited to the spectacular Blenheim Palace, home of his cousin, the Duke of Marlborough. The visit was set for 10 August, a week before he was due to go and stay with Violet at Slains Castle. It didn't take a genius to work out that it wasn't going to end well for one of the two women.

Soon after Clementine arrived at Blenheim Palace, Winston proposed to her, and she readily accepted his proposal. It was decided that the engagement should be announced on 15 August, two days before Churchill was due to go and stay with Violet at Slains Castle. Violet didn't even know of Clementine's existence, let alone the fact that she was the woman who was destined to be marrying Winston and not her.

There are some who suggest that the only reason Churchill became involved with Violet was to secure favour with her father. Although at the time it was still some seven months before he became the British prime minister, it was no secret that Herbert Asquith would ultimately have the position bestowed upon him. As with all such appointments, new people are always brought in by the incoming prime minister, people who he feels he can trust, people he will need around to keep him and his government strong. It would appear that Churchill wanted to be one of those men, and that he saw Violet as his way of securing his place amongst Asquith's inner circle. The other consideration for Churchill was whether Clementine would turn down his wedding proposal? What would he have done then? Would he have carried on seeing Violet and eventually married her?

I don't believe his behaviour in this matter showed Churchill in a good light, and certainly wasn't one of the best decisions he ever made. Neither Violet nor Clementine were casual affairs or simple dalliances; he had clearly seen both women as potential wives and had grown close to them both at the same time, knowing full well he was going to let one of them down. Even allowing for his awkwardness around women, his treatment of Violet, in particular, was incomprehensible. Although publicly she said all the right things and was both understanding and supportive of Churchill and Clementine's marriage, privately she was as hurt as any wronged woman would have been.

Before his engagement to Clementine was announced, he felt it only right that he contacted Violet to tell her that he would not be coming up to see her at Slains Castle as promised, which he did by sending her a note. But at the risk of incurring Clementine's wrath, Churchill did eventually go and visit Violet. On Monday, 24 August 1908, he caught a train from King's Cross to visit Violet, with whom he stayed for a week, before returning to London and Clementine, who, fortunately for Churchill, was still waiting for him.

Despite her treatment by Churchill being less than chivalrous, Violet still had fond memories of him. Two months after he and Clementine were married, he arranged for all three of them to meet up for lunch in London. As might be imagined it was a somewhat subdued occasion. But as was the norm of their class, dirty laundry was rarely washed in public, because it was just not the thing to do. Despite her feelings for Churchill, Violet played the game and kept her own counsel.

She continued to support Churchill from afar in his political life.

Chapter 3

Miners in Tonypandy (1910)

Quite simply the miners in Tonypandy had had enough. They had been pushed too far, and a strike was inevitable. Their actions were an attempt to improve wages and living conditions for them and their families who lived in the town, which in 1910 was a severely deprived area of South Wales, where the mining industry was one of the region's biggest employers.

Churchill was the Home Secretary at the time of the riots, and he did himself no favours at Tonypandy, or throughout South Wales for that matter, in fact the ill feeling towards him that began back then runs so deep that it still simmers to this very day.

Miners' wages in Tonypandy and throughout South Wales had been deliberately kept low for many years, because the owners of the different coal mines worked together as the Cambrian Combine, for their own financial benefit, to ensure that this remained the case. This is what led to the Rhondda riots of 1910. There were a series of violent confrontations between the striking coal miners and the police, which took place at different locations throughout the Rhondda mines in South Wales.

The Ely Pit in the village of Penygraig in Glamorgan was owned by the Naval Colliery Company and in late August 1910 a new coal seam was opened at the pit. Although there was always initial excitement at such new discoveries, the reality of how viable such new seams would be soon had to be considered. But in the case of this new coal seam, the owners of the pit claimed that the miners who had initially worked on the seam had purposely worked as slowly as they possibly could. This included a team of seventy men, who refuted the owners' allegations and argued that they hadn't purposely worked slowly, but that the new seam was harder to work because there was a band of stone running through it, which determined how fast they could work.

The owners, Naval Colliery Company, did not accept the miners' explanation and on 1 September 1910 they placed a lockout notice, or a notification of a temporary work stoppage, on the colliery's main gates, and closed the mine. This action wasn't just against the 70 men who had been working the new seam, but the mine's entire 950 workers. The angry miners at the Ely Pit responded by going on strike. Rather than indulging in sensible dialogue, the owners did no more than bring in miners from outside the area who were prepared to come and work at Ely. These were often referred to as 'strike breakers'.

Ely miners reacted by picketing their pit, so the situation quickly worsened. On 1 November 1910, the South Wales Miners' Federation, balloted all their members, which resulted in the 12,000 members who worked at mines owned by the Cambrian Combine all going out on strike. This wasn't what the owners had anticipated at all. They had most probably seen an opportunity to strengthen their own position but the stance they took quickly backfired on them. With all of their pits closed they were not making any money, so a Board of Conciliation was quickly established so that an agreement could be reached, the men could go back to work and the owners could once again start earning money. William Abraham, a bull of a man, and just as fierce-looking, represented the miners. An agreed wage of 2s 3d per ton was agreed upon, but it was with some surprise that the miners rejected the offer and stayed out on strike.

Besides being a trade unionist, William Abraham was also the MP for Rhondda. Between 1885 and 1910, he had represented the Liberal Party, but in the January 1910 general election he had joined the Labour Party.

The longer the strike went on, the more concern grew about what was going to happen, especially as it was clear that 'temperatures' amongst the miners were growing.

The troubles at the pits owned by the Cambrian Combine were made worse by another nearby strike at neighbouring Cynon Valley, an area between Rhondda and the Merthyr Valley.

On Sunday, 6 November 1910, the Chief Constable of Glamorgan sent some 200 police officers into the Tonypandy area, where, because of the strike, even mines owned by other companies were closed. Only one, the Llwynypia Colliery was open. That same day, striking miners became aware that the owners of Llwynypia intended to bring in strike breakers, to carry out maintenance work on the air pumps and ventilation pumps.

The following morning, striking miners turned up at Llwynypia Colliery and picketed it to prevent the strike breakers from entering to carry out the necessary work. A small group of the strikers seemed hell-bent on violence, and after stoning the pump house they broke down a wooden fence that surrounded the pit and began fighting with police officers who had been stationed inside the colliery. The police eventually managed to force the miners out of the colliery by repeatedly mounting baton charges, and pushed them all the way back to Tonypandy Square. Between 1 and 2am the following morning there was a demonstration by striking miners, which was eventually dispersed by Cardiff police officers using batons – but not before there were casualties on both sides. This was the last straw for Lionel Lindsay, the Chief Constable of Glamorgan Constabulary, who decided to contact the War Office and ask for military support. His request was backed up by the general manager of the Cambrian Combine, not that there was any collusion between the two.

Lindsay's request for military assistance came to the notice of Winston Churchill, the Home Secretary, who, to his credit on this occasion, intervened. He turned down the initial request as he felt that the local authorities were overreacting to the situation. But I don't believe this was out of any concern for the well-being of the miners and their families, it was simply because, by trying to prevent matters from escalating, he saw a way of making political gain for the Liberal Party, and no doubt himself. What Churchill did do was to send members of the Metropolitan Police, some of whom were from the Force's mounted section. Although he held back from deploying cavalry, instead of sending some them to stand by at Cardiff, he authorised civil authorities to use them if they saw fit to do so.

Trying to appear caring and consolatory to the miners, Churchill personally told them that for the time being he had only sent police and was holding back on the soldiers. Whether that was said as a threat, or in a way which might suggest that he cared about their plight, is unclear. Later in the day, the mood had changed sufficiently for the local Stipendiary to send a telegram to London with a request for military support, which was approved by the Home Office, and troops were deployed, despite Churchill's assurance that they were only sending in the police for the time being.

On the evening of Tuesday, 8 November 1910, rioting took place in Tonypandy, with many businesses having their windows smashed. There was no mass outbreak of looting, although some took place.

There had been a meeting at the Mid-Rhondda Athletic Ground earlier in the day, where there had been a large turnout – measured in the thousands. After the meeting, a procession was formed and the crowd, predominantly made up of men, decided to march. They started down Dunraven Street in Tonypandy, then headed off towards Miskin, making their way through Trealaw and on to Llwynypia, to the Glamorgan Pits. This was where the march came to an end with most of the men remaining near the entrance to the colliery yard. For nearly an hour they stood there chatting amongst themselves. There was no aggression, no violence, not even acts of agitation, but that all changed at about 5.30pm, when a group of youths began throwing stones at the power station, gradually smashing all the front-facing windows of the building. The police were called and mounted police galloped up the road with batons drawn attacking the miners as they rode. The crowds were so hefty in size there came a point when the mounted police could go no further, so they turned round and charged back down the road until they reached the relative safety of the entrance to the power station. But on the way they had to make their way through the same crowds, who this time were waiting for them, armed with stones and other such implements. Thankfully for the police and their horses, none of them were seriously injured.

For ammunition and implements with which they could protect themselves from the baton-wielding police, some of the crowd tore down a large advertising hoarding near the Thistle Hotel, Llwynypia, and the broken timber from the hoardings was used as staves for protection against the police. Also, a large brick and stone pillar opposite the hotel was pulled down and the debris, to be used as missiles against the police and for smashing windows, was thrown across the road.

The Chief Constable, Captain Lionel Lindsay, spoke to the strikers outside the main entrance of the colliery yard, asking them to have respect and regard for colliery property, and to disperse quietly and make their way home. But they didn't. Instead, the striking miners proceeded to demolish what remained of the wooden fencing enclosing the colliery yard, the debris of which was strewn across the roadway, which in turn stopped the tram network. All the street lights in the road immediately outside the colliery were completely wrecked and the lights extinguished. But it didn't stop there. All the windows in the colliery offices were completely smashed.

Subsequently the striking miners concentrated their attention on the Glamorgan Colliery power station, and the police had to perform repeated baton charges to prevent the attack. Even the colliery management managed to keep the machines running.

Shortly before 6pm, the tone of the rioting changed for the worse, and urgent messages were sent to the workmen's committee, which was sitting at the Rickards Hall in Tonypandy, in the hope that some of them would come to the scene and try and appease the striking miners. The committee thought the request serious enough to suspend their meeting and make their way to the colliery, but by 7pm the road from the Glamorgan Colliery entrance as far as Tonypandy Square, a distance of a quarter of a mile, was completely blocked, so large were the crowds. Police officers, in the form of those from the Metropolitan Police arrived in Tonypandy Town Square at around 10.30pm, some three hours after the rioting had begun.

At least one shop was left alone and sustained no damage to it at all. The shop in question was owned by Willie Llewellyn, who was the town's pharmacist, and ex-Wales and British Lion Rugby Union player. He first represented Wales against England in 1899, going on to represent his country on twenty occasions and last playing for them in 1905. His four appearances for the British Lions all came in 1904 on the tour of Australasia.

The police seemed more concerned about protecting the homes of the mine owners and managers than they did the business properties in Tonypandy town centre. Cavalry of the 18th Hussars were eventually deployed on 9 November, but simply carried out proactive patrols. During the riots, soldiers from the Lancashire Fusiliers were brought into the area and billeted at Llwynypia.

Once the situation had calmed down, it was established that eighty police officers had been injured. Figures for the miners were harder to establish, as many did not seek medical assistance through fear of being identified and prosecuted by the authorities. In total, thirteen miners from the village of Gilfach Goch were prosecuted for the part they played in the riots. The trial took six days. Some were found guilty and received custodial sentences of between two and six weeks, some were fined, whilst others were discharged.

All the business premises in the main thoroughfare of Tonypandy were barricaded on the evening of Wednesday, 9 November 1910, some with planks laid onto the window frames and others with sheets of corrugated iron. Tons of broken plate glass cumbered the streets, and the police were engaged in clearing away the debris and removing what might, in the event of a further outbreak of hostilities, be converted into ammunition by the rioters.

The clearance had its funny side. Metropolitan police constables, all men of fine physique and accustomed to patrolling the streets of London, were seen stooping over debris working away with shovels for dear life, and appearing to enjoy the occupation. One of the constables was overheard to say, 'I have been in one or two rough and tumbles with the suffragettes, but, my word, you're hot stuff at Tonypandy.'

The Hussars made their appearance in Rhondda about 12.30pm the same day, and the troops presented a beautiful spectacle. Thousands of people lined the main streets from Tonypandy and Penygraig to Llwynypia station as the men passed through the main centre of the village. The soldiers patrolled the streets, and especially the roads surrounding the position occupied by the 'stone bombers' on the previous two nights, immediately facing the Glamorgan Colliery. Some of the strikers could be heard shouting out, 'are we disheartened?' to which the vociferous response was a firm 'No.'

The soldiers were taunted with such sarcastic remarks as, 'Can you shoot straight?' but they kept their thoughts to themselves and did not respond. Despite this there was no out-and-out animosity from the local people towards the soldiers.

All the way from the bottom of Tonypandy to the Llwynypia Baths, where the cavalry were quartered at the time, they were subjected to a great deal of banter as they made their way along the road. One amongst the soldiers who was not in uniform, believed to be a groom, came in for some stick. 'There's a blackleg amongst them,' one of the crowd remarked, much to everybody's amusement.

The Hussars had in fact already left Tonypandy for Pontypridd, a convenient centre from which to enter any of the valleys where their services might have been required. Their place had been taken by the North Lancashire and Lancashire Fusiliers.

At 11pm on the evening of Wednesday, 9 November 1910, Tonypandy was quiet, but despite this the police still continued to patrol the streets, and were at times subjected to jeers and boos by gangs of youths, but the constables took everything in their stride, and other than the odd smile and nod of the head, they did not respond or take the bait.

The *Sunderland Daily Echo* newspaper dated Thursday, 10 November 1910, included a 'communication' from the Home Office. It read as follows:

> Reports from every part of Rhonnda Valley are satisfactory. At Porth, where the licensed houses had not been closed, there was some slight disorder, which is now under control. The Chief Constable had now received the third contingent of 300 Metropolitan Police despatched at 4pm yesterday from London, and he therefore has at his disposal more than 1,400 constables. The town of Tonypandy is under complete control, and the work of bringing up the imprisoned horses at the colliery has already commenced. No loss of life is reported from the district, and for the present a much quieter feeling prevails. No further movements of the military are necessary while the Police have the situation so thoroughly in hand. General Macready will, however, remain at Tonypandy for the night.

> The Home Secretary [Winston Churchill] has expressed his appreciation of the discipline and good spirit which the Police have shown in circumstances of exceptional difficulty. Their efforts have made it possible so far to avoid the use of military force. While it would be premature to conclude that danger of disturbance is past, there can be no doubt of the ability of the authorities to restrain disorder with the forces at their disposal.

An interesting exchange took place between the Miners' Federation and the Home Secretary, Winston Churchill, in correspondence dated 9 November 1910.

Dear Sir,

At a conference of the Miners' Federation of Great Britain held today at the Westminster Palace Hotel in London, the following resolution was passed unanimously, and I was instructed to send it to you.

I am yours very truly

Thomas Ashton

Secretary.

That this conference, having heard the report of the South Wales representatives regarding the serious situation which has arisen in South Wales, whilst regretting the disturbances which have occurred, consider the civil forces sufficient to deal with such disturbances, and will strongly deprecate the employment of the military for such purpose, and, if the military have been sent into the districts affected, asks the Home Secretary, at once to recall them.

Home Office

London November 9th.

Dear Sir,

I am desired by the Home Secretary to acknowledge the receipt of your letter and resolution. Mr Churchill hopes and expects that the strong force of Police drafted to the scene of the disorder will be sufficient, promptly and effectively to prevent riot. If, however, this is not so he will not hesitate, after what has occurred, to authorise the employment of the military, and the responsibility for any consequences which may ensue must rest with those who persist in courses of violence.

Yours faithfully

S W Harris.

A newspaper report appeared in *The Scotsman* on Friday, 28 July 1911, in relation to two of those who were charged and put before the courts.

> A Stipendiary had before him a Danger of Life case arising out of Tuesday's rioting at Tonypandy. William Lowis Jones, a grocer's assistant, was charged at Porth yesterday with assaulting the Police, and was fined £8 or one month's imprisonment. The accused who appeared in court with a blood stained bandage around his head, denied that he threw stones, but the Stipendiary remarked that respectable people should not mix in disorderly crowds. All who were with the crowd were really aiding and abetting. Alfred Lewis, against whom a similar charge was preferred, was sentenced to six weeks imprisonment with hard labour. The Stipendiary said amongst foreigners the use of the knife was a practice requiring suppression, but in this country a new danger to life had arisen, stone throwing.

One miner, Samuel Rhys, died during the riots the result of head injuries. The following was the decision of the coroner's jury:

> We agree that Samuel Rhys died from injuries he received on November 8 caused by some blunt instrument. The evidence is not sufficiently clear to us how he received those injuries.

The medical evidence was similar in that it found that Samuel Rhys died as a result of a fractured skull caused by a blunt instrument. 'It might have been caused by a Policeman's truncheon or by two of the several weapons used by the strikers which were produced in court.'

Although there was no specific evidence against any individual police officer having struck Samuel, to try and infer that his injuries were caused by other miners seems somewhat at odds with the actual events.

The striking miners returned to work in early September 1911, a year after the original lockout which started the riots in the first place.

Somewhat ironically the troops behaved better than the local and Metropolitan Police did, and they were also viewed somewhat differently and better than the police officers were. What also annoyed the miners and their families was that although there was no particular gripe towards the military for any specific acts of aggression, it was the very presence of the soldiers which had prevented them from striking, which in turn prolonged the strike much longer than it needed to be and so reduced the chance of the strike ending in the miners' favour.

There were those in the community who felt Winston Churchill didn't do enough to bring the riots to an end earlier. This in itself shows how great the social divide was back in 1910, between the haves and the have-nots. Mr Leonard Llewellyn, general manager of the Cambrian Combine, stated in an interview that there were plenty of winding enginemen ready to come to work, but they had been frightened by the crowds. All kinds of threats had been used to intimidate them. Their wives were terrorised and notes had been thrust beneath their doors containing threats to kill them if they ventured to the power station. Mr Llewellyn criticised the action of the Home Secretary, Winston Churchill, in holding back the military, and said it was only when it was discovered that the military were being stopped that the rioting commenced.

Mr David Alfred Thomas, who would later become The Viscount Rhondda, was in 1910, the MP for Cardiff, having previously represented Merthyr Tydfil between 1888 and 1910. As the head of the Cambrian Combine, he expressed his regret that the request of the Chief Constable of Glamorgan for the deployment of troops in the area had not been complied with earlier. He quoted the experience in the hauliers' strike of 1893, adding that it showed clearly the direct effect that just the very presence of an adequate military force had upon the more reckless and turbulent spirits of strikers and large non-compliant crowds. The police, he said, had acted admirably and it was impossible to praise their conduct too highly, but it was not fair to subject them to being assaulted by such men, whilst arming them with only batons.

It is interesting to note that besides being an MP, Thomas was also a very wealthy man, having inherited his father's coalmining business. During the First World War he was on board the RMS *Lusitania* when it was torpedoed by a German submarine and sank on 7 May 1915. Both he and his daughter, Margaret were amongst the survivors.

The defeat of the miners in 1911 was seen by the workers, their families and the local community, as being down to state intervention by

Churchill and his government. There were those in Wales who saw his reaction of sending the military into their country as a total overreaction to what was actually taking place.

In 1940, when Chamberlain's wartime government was struggling and Winston Churchill's new government took over, he needed the support of the other political parties. Clement Atlee, the leader of the Labour Party, said that they might not be able to offer their support to him due to his association with Tonypandy.

During the 1950 general election campaign, when Churchill gave a speech in Cardiff, the troubles of Tonypandy were once again brought up and used against him, forcing him to defend himself over the matter.

> When I was Home Secretary in 1910, I had a great horror
> and fear of having to become responsible for the military
> firing on a crowd of rioters and strikers. Also, I was always
> in sympathy with the miners.

There are many people in Wales, at the time and now, who do not believe that statement.

Chapter 4

Gallipoli 1915

Without doubt, one of Winston Churchill's biggest mistakes came about in 1915, when as the Lord of the Admiralty, he decided to attack Turkey along the Dardanelles peninsula. It was a campaign that continued for eight and a half months and involved the deployment of about 1 million troops.

Gallipoli was a military failure, a national humiliation, and an end to Churchill's wartime political career. The level of just how big a failure the campaign was could easily be measured by the fact that he was removed from his Cabinet post, lost his position on the War Council, and was allowed no further part in wartime military decisions.

In later life, even Churchill recognised that Gallipoli was a tragedy, not necessarily for those who took part in it and suffered as a result, but for his own political career. I'm not sure that describes a man who has regrets for the right reasons. At the time of Gallipoli, Churchill was still only 39 years old, and already set in his ways. He was, by nature, a stubborn individual, who once he had set his mind on moving in a certain direction, wasn't great at deviating from where he wanted to go, possibly because he saw it as a weakness, or worried that others might think of him as being indecisive. The problem with being stubborn is it very rarely leaves any room for manoeuvre, even when it is clear that the initial idea, plan or strategy, could have been approached in a slightly different way, and have had more productive outcomes. Unfortunately the loss of a man's life wasn't always a deterrent to prevent a bad idea from becoming a nightmare reality.

Gallipoli should never have taken place: plain and simple. At the time Churchill was Lord of the Admiralty, the First Sea Lord was John Arbuthnot Fisher. He had served in the Royal Navy for fifty-six years between 1854 and 1910, when he retired on reaching his sixty-ninth birthday. At the time he had been the First Sea Lord for seven years. He was brought back onto the active list, once again as First Sea Lord, in November 1914.

Fisher wasn't a warrior in the sense that he wasn't a sea-going admiral who directed and fought in major sea battles, he was more of a strategist and an innovator. In 1904, soon after becoming the First Sea Lord, he took 150 ships out of service as he felt that they were no longer fit for operational purposes. In their place he produced a modern up to date navy; one which was ready and able to meet the challenges ahead.

He looked at ways of making a ship's guns more effective, in all aspects, as well as having the foresight to recognise the importance that submarines would play in future warfare. He was largely responsible for changing British naval vessels from coal-driven to oil-fuelled. He also helped progress the development of torpedo boat destroyers in the Royal Navy. In 1908, he predicted the beginning of the First World War being in October 1914.

So Winston Churchill had Fisher as his 'wing man' and when told by him, in plain simple English, that the plan for Gallipoli was not only not going to work, but was fraught with the possibility that it would be an utter disaster, did Churchill listen? No, he didn't. Instead he pushed on with his plan convinced for some insane reason it would work. All it did achieve was the loss of tens of thousands of British and Allied troops' lives. British fighting casualties, dead and wounded, totalled 160,790, with a further 3,778 dying of disease, whilst a further 90,000 were evacuated from the peninsula due to sickness and disease.

Why was there a need for a Gallipoli-type campaign in the first place? Because the Western Front had become a stalemate and bogged down in trench warfare. The First Battle of the Marne, which took place between 6 and 12 September 1914, and which resulted in 13,000 British casualties, was later followed by the First Battle of Ypres, between 19 October and 22 November 1914, resulting in some 57,000 British casualties.

An added part of the equation was that the Russian leader, Grand Duke Nicholas, had asked Britain for assistance against the Ottoman Empire which had begun an offensive against the Russians in the Caucasus region.

The political fallout began whilst the campaign was still underway, when on 15 May 1915, Fisher resigned as the First Sea Lord, the result of fierce arguments with Churchill over Gallipoli – which ultimately resulted in Churchill's resignation as well. Fisher had preferred an amphibious attack on the German Baltic Sea coastline (known as the Baltic Plan) where substantial forces would land on the flat beaches of Pomerania, which was not even 100 miles from the German capital in Berlin. To support the amphibious assault, Fisher's plan required a selection of 600 naval vessels, a number of which would be used to keep the Imperial German Navy from effectively intervening. The plan was never activated.

Sir Ian Hamilton, who was the commander of the Mediterranean Expeditionary Force, was recalled to London in October 1915, which resulted in his military career coming to an abrupt end.

Prime Minister Herbert Asquith was forced to end his Liberal government as a result of the political fallout over Gallipoli, and form a coalition government with the Conservative Party. Asquith also decided on setting up a commission into the failings at Gallipoli. An interim report was issued in 1917 with the final report being published in 1919.

The investigation into the Dardanelles Campaign, which was set up under the Special Commissions (Dardanelles and Mesopotamia) Act 1915, found major problems with the planning and execution of the campaign.

The members of the Commission were a distinguished bunch of gentlemen. It was chaired by Sir William Pickford, a lawyer and a judge, who later became the 1st Baron Sterndale. Other members included the Earl of Cromer, who was a diplomat and a colonial administrator; Mr Andrew Fisher, who between 1908 and 1915 served three separate terms as the Australian prime minister; Thomas Mackenzie, former prime minister of New Zealand; Sir Frederick Cawley, chancellor of the Duchy of Lancaster; Lord Clyde, privy counsellor; Mr Stephen Gwynn, MP for Galway; Mr Walter Roch, MP for Pembrokeshire; Sir William May, Admiral of the Fleet, and Field Marshal Lord Nicholson.

The Parliamentary Commission's report into the Dardanelles campaign was first published in 1917, and concluded that it had been fatally compromised by a number of factors. The difficulties of a military attack on the peninsula were severely under-estimated and insufficient resources were diverted from the Western Front to ensure its success. Both of the Allied landings on the peninsula, in April and August 1915, were flawed. The commission also censured by name a number of high ranking military figures, most notably Sir Ian Hamilton.

The Commission came up with sixteen conclusions, which included the following:

> (1). We think that when it was decided to undertake an important military expedition to the Gallipoli Peninsula, sufficient consideration was not given to the measures necessary to carry out such an expedition with success. We have already pointed out in paragraph 15 that it had been apparent in February 1915 that serious military operations might be necessary. Under these circumstances we think that the conditions of a military attack on the Peninsula should have been studied and a general plan prepared by the Chief of the Imperial General Staff, Sir James Wolfe Murray, special attention being paid to the probable effect of naval gun fire in support of the troops; and that it was the duty of the Secretary of State for War to ensure this was done.

It was quite staggering to think that a military operation of such a magnitude wasn't looked into in much more detail. Why the Secretary of State for War failed in his duty to ensure a general plan for the operation was prepared was not explained, neither was the reason why no action was taken against the Chief of the Imperial General Staff.

> (2). We think that the difficulties of the operation were much underestimated. At the outset all decisions were taken and all provisions based on the assumption that, if a landing were effected, the resistance would be slight and the advance rapid. We can see no sufficient ground for this assumption. The short naval bombardment in November 1914 had given the Turks warning of a possible attack, and the naval operations in February and March 1915 led naturally to a great strengthening of the Turkish defences. The Turks were known to be led by German officers, and there was

no reason to think that they would not fight well, especially in defensive positions. These facts had been reported by Admiral de Roebeck and Sir Ian Hamilton.

Not for the first time the arrogance of senior military personnel, and politicians in this case, cost fighting men their lives. It makes absolutely no sense whatsoever, why it should have been felt that Turkish soldiers wouldn't have been anything other than well trained and dedicated to the cause in defending their homeland when called upon to do so against an invading army.

Why naval bombardments of the Gallipoli peninsula were carried out, other than immediately before an amphibious landing, simply beggars belief. All it did was give prior warning of such an attack being imminent, which allowed the Turks to increase their military resources in the area, along with strengthening and adding to their defensive positions.

> (3). We think that the position which, in fact, existed after the first attacks in April and the early days of May should have been regarded from the outset as possible and the requisite means of meeting it considered. This would have made it necessary to examine and decide whether the demands of such extended operations could be met consistently with our obligations in other theatres of war. In fact those obligations made it impossible in May, June and July to supply the forces with the necessary drafts, gun ammunition, high explosives and other modern appliances of war.

This I believe is yet another example of British arrogance. The question of long term sustainability in relation to the aftermath of such an invasion does not seem to have been properly considered. It is almost as if they expected an immediate victory due to little or no resistance. They simply hadn't considered there would be a long-term need for the supply of men, ammunition and equipment.

> (4). We are of the opinion that, with the resources then available, success in the Dardanelles, if possible, was only possible upon condition that the government concentrated

their efforts upon the enterprise and limited their expenditure of men and material in the Western theatre of war. This condition was never fulfilled.

At the risk of repeating myself, this is yet another case of arrogance by British government ministers and senior military personnel. Nobody appears to have even perceived the slightest possibility that there might have been the need for any additional men or equipment to help support the resources that were initially used in the landings on the Dardanelles Peninsula.

> (5). After the failure of the attacks which followed the first landing there was undue delay in deciding upon the course to be pursued in the future. Sir Ian Hamilton's appreciation was forwarded on 17 May 1915. It was not considered by the War Council or the Cabinet until 7 June. The reconstruction of the government which took place at this most critical period was the main cause of the delay. As a consequence the despatch of the reinforcements asked for by Sir Ian Hamilton in his appreciation was postponed for six weeks.

Whilst the War Council and the Cabinet were doing whatever it was they were doing, and despite a government reconstruction at the time, between 17 May and 7 June 1915, 3,933 officers and men of the British and Commonwealth forces involved in the Gallipoli campaign were killed in action or died of their wounds, illness or disease.

> (6). We think that the plan of attack from Anzac and Suvla in the beginning of August was open to criticism. The terrain over which the attack had to be made was very difficult, especially at Anzac. In order to obtain if possible the element of surprise, the main advance of the Anzac force up the north-western spurs of Sari Bahr was undertaken at night, the risk of misdirection and failure was much increased by doing so. The plan however, was decided upon after a consideration of other plans, and with the concurrence of the commander of the Anzac Corps, who had been in command since the first landing.

It would appear that the landings at both Anzac Cove and Suvla Bay, were undertaken without any previous knowledge of what the terrain they would encounter would be like once they had made their way inland off the beaches. As if that wasn't bad enough, to then have a large part of the invading force undertake a night-time march over such terrain, would be laughable if it wasn't so potentially life-threatening for those who had to undertake it.

> (7). The operations at Suvla were a severe trial for a force consisting of troops who had never been under fire, but we think that after taking into consideration and making every allowance for the difficulties of the attack and the inexperience of the troops, the attack was not pressed as it should have been at Suvla on the 7th and 8th August, and we attribute this in a great measure to a want of determination and competence in the Divisional Commander and one of his Brigadiers. The leading of the 11th Division and the attached Battalions of the 10th Division, which constituted the main body of the attack, was not satisfactory. As explained in paragraphs 108 and 109, the orders given by General Hammersley were confused and the work of his staff, defective. Major-General Hammersley's health had in the past been such that it was dangerous to select him for a divisional command in the field, although he seemed to have recovered. We think that the defects that we have mentioned in his leading probably arose from this cause. General Sitwell, the senior Brigade Commander, did not, in our opinion, show sufficient energy and decision making.

If ever there was an incorrect combination, this was it. It is absolutely astounding that anybody could determine that inexperienced troops taking part in what for them was their baptism of fire, were not be led by experienced, practical and exemplary leaders.

> (8). Sir Frederick Stopford was hampered by the want of effective leading above referred to, and the inexperience of his troops, but we do not think he took sufficient means to

inform himself of the progress of operations. On August 7th, when he became aware that the troops had not advanced as rapidly as had been intended, we think that he should have asked for some explanation from General Hammersley. In that case he would have been informed of the difference which had arisen between General Sitwell and General Hill, and of General Sitwell's lack of vigour and energy in leading. We think that at this point his intervention was needed.

We think that he and his staff were partly responsible for the failure to supply the troops with water on August 7th and 8th. Our detailed conclusions on the water supply will be found below.

We cannot endorse Sir Ian Hamilton's condemnation of the orders given by Sir Frederick Stopford on the morning of August 8th, 1915, whether the account of them given in Sir Ian Hamilton's despatch or that in Sir Frederick Stopford's report to him be accepted. According to the evidence of Sir Bryan Mahon and General Hammersley they were not deterred from advancing by those orders.

On the evening of August 8th we think that Sir Frederick Stopford's difficulties were increased by the intervention of Sir Ian Hamilton. Sir Ian Hamilton seems to have considered Sir Frederick Stopford lacking in energy in the operations between August 9th and August 15th. As this opinion is based more upon general conduct than upon any specific acts or omissions, we are not in a position to pronounce upon it. We realise, however, that importance attaches to the impressions of a Commander-in-Chief on such a subject.

How is it possible that so many senior military personnel who were either under-performing or simply not up to the task at hand, were involved in any kind of actual military operation, let alone the same one? How could it be that it took an operation such as Gallipoli to discover their operational shortcomings?

(9). As regards Sir Ian Hamilton it is inevitable that the capabilities of a commander in war should be judged by the results he achieves, even though, if these results are disappointing, his failure may be due to causes for which he is only partially responsible.

In April, 1915, Sir Ian Hamilton succeeded in landing his troops at the places which he had chosen; but the operations that were intended immediately to follow the landing were abruptly checked owing to a miscalculation of the strength of the Turkish defences and the fighting qualities of the Turkish troops. This rebuff should have convinced Sir Ian Hamilton that the Turkish entrenchments were skilfully disposed and well-armed, and that naval gun fire was ineffective against trenches and entanglements of the modern type. We doubt however, whether the failure of these operations sufficiently impressed Sir Ian Hamilton and the military authorities at home with the serious nature of the opposition likely to be encountered.

During May, June and July severe fighting took place, but its results were not commensurate with the efforts made and the losses incurred.

During July a plan of combined operations was elaborated, which was carried into effect early in August. Sir Ian Hamilton was confident of success, but was again baffled by the obstinacy of the Turkish resistance. Moreover the failure of night advances in a difficult and unexplored country, which formed part of the plan, led to heavy casualties and temporarily disorganised the forces employed.

Sir Ian Hamilton was relieved of his command on October 15th.

We recognise Sir Ian Hamilton's personal gallantry and energy, his sanguine disposition, and his determination to win at all costs. We recognise also that the task entrusted to him was one of extreme difficulty, the more so as the authorities at home at first misconceived the nature and duration of the operations, and afterwards were slow to realise that to drive the Turks out of their entrenchments and occupy the heights commanding the Straits was a formidable and hazardous enterprise which demanded a concentration of force and effort. It must further be borne in mind that Lord Kitchener, whom Sir Ian Hamilton appears to have regarded as a Commander-in-Chief rather than a Secretary of State, pressed upon him the paramount importance, if it were by any means possible, of carrying out the task assigned to him.

Though from time to time, Sir Ian Hamilton represented the need of drafts, reinforcements, guns and munitions, which the government found it impossible to supply, he was nevertheless always ready to renew the struggle with the resources at his disposal, and to the last was confident of success. For this it would be hard to blame him; but viewing the Expedition in the light of events it would, in our opinion, have been well had he examined the situation as disclosed by the first landings in a more critical spirit, impartially weighed the probabilities of success and failure, having regard to the resources in men and material which could be placed at his disposal, and submitted to the Secretary of State for War a comprehensive statement of the arguments for and against a continuance of the operations.

In fairness to Sir Ian Hamilton, it would appear that he tried his hardest, and acted to the best of his abilities in what can only be described as extremely difficult circumstances.

(10). The failure at Anzac was due mainly to the difficulties of the country (Terrain) and the strength of the enemy. The failure at Suvla also prevented any pressure being put upon the Turkish forces in that direction, and success at Suvla might have lessened the resistance at Anzac.

(11). We think that after the attacks ending on August 9th had failed, the operations contemplated could not have been successfully carried out without large reinforcements. The fighting after General de Lisle replaced Sir Frederick Stopford was really of a defensive character.

It is quite possible that by now there was an understanding by those in high command that a continuation of the campaign was pointless. The potential of further and unnecessary losses had to be weighed up against a continued effort to positively progress matters, whilst at the same time saving face for the Empire, nation and individual reputations.

> (12). We think that after the advice of Sir Charles Monro had been confirmed by Lord Kitchener, the decision to evacuate should have been taken at once. We recognise however, that the question of evacuation was connected with other questions of high policy which do not appear to us to come within the scope of our enquiry.

Always a difficult decision no matter who had to make it, but once again, the longer it took to take, the more severe the consequences became. Sufficient numbers of vessels had to be found to carry out the evacuations, the operation had to be undertaken without the Turkish forces becoming aware, and a location or locations had to be agreed upon where all of the evacuated soldiers could be taken to, before they were either sent home to the United Kingdom or forwarded on to another theatre of war.

> (13). We think that the decision to evacuate when taken was right.

> (14). We think that operations were hampered throughout by the failure to supply sufficient artillery and munitions, and to keep the original formations up to strength by the provision of adequate drafts as well as reinforcements. In our opinion this was not owing to any neglect on the part of the Heads of Departments charged with such provision, but to the demands proving much larger than was expected when the operations were undertaken and to demands which had to be met in other theatres of war.

On the other hand, a considerable amount of artillery was available in Egypt and at Mudros for the Suvla operations, but it was not utilised.

The first question to ask here is why were so many available artillery pieces not deployed to the Dardanelles Peninsula, but instead left in Egypt and Mudros, as it just makes no sense at all. Secondly, despite the Commission stating there was no neglect on the part of the heads of departments charged with the provision for adequate drafts and reinforcements, some responsibility must lay at their feet because of their positions. Despite the allowances, or excuses, made by the Commission (you decide which), a commander has a responsibility to his men to try his best on their behalf, and it would appear on this occasion, this didn't happen.

(15). Many minor frontal attacks were made without adequate artillery preparation, which produced little or no material advantage. Evidence was given that these attacks entailed an unnecessary loss of life. Without a more intimate knowledge of the locality and conditions than it is possible for us to obtain, we cannot express an opinion as to whether it was right to undertake such attacks. We think that the evidence disproves the allegation made before us that useless attacks were made because of the neglect on the part of superior Commanders and Staff Officers to visit and inspect the trenches and positions.

The comments made by the commission on this point seem somewhat strange. Does it really matter what terrain men were running over in a direct frontal assault on enemy defensive positions? By their very nature such attacks would result in a high loss of life, and if the actual gain made was marginal, then any loss of life is always going to be questionable.

(16) There was full co-operation between the Navy and the Army and the two services worked well and harmoniously together.

The first thing I noticed whilst reading through the Commission's report into the Dardanelles campaign, is that none of the conclusions make any mention or reference to Winston Churchill, but that doesn't mean for one second that he was blameless for the failings of the operation. That would be like saying that because Adolf Hitler wasn't present at, or mentioned during, the Wannsee Conference in Berlin on 20 January 1942, he was not responsible for the Holocaust during the Second World War.

What suddenly becomes extremely amazing was how Churchill managed to get his plan for Gallipoli past the War Department in the first place. It was poorly planned, lacked sufficient artillery pieces, many of the troops deployed were inexperienced and many had no actual fighting experience. Many of the maps that British commanders had were inaccurate. Allied intelligence about numbers of enemy troops and equipment was poor, meaning that British commanders were not absolutely sure what they were up against. It became clear that certain senior officers were not quite up to the job. Fisher had tried his best to get other senior officers to see sense and realise how bad the plan was, but he failed. One of the things that become apparent was the level of British arrogance. It was almost as if the British believed that all they had to do was to turn up, disembark and the Turkish troops, who were not considered to be 'worthy opponents', would either surrender or run away.

Churchill had even considered using sulfur mustard or mustard gas, as it was more commonly referred to, in the Gallipoli campaign against Ottoman troops, but didn't. Germany went on to become the first nation to use it in July 1917, prior to the Third Battle of Ypres. The use of mustard gas wasn't with intent to kill the enemy, although if used in concentrated enough doses, it could most definitely kill. Its main purpose was to incapacitate. It caused internal and external bleeding and attacked the bronchial tubes, the results of which were extremely painful. Externally it resulted in those affected by its use to suffer enormous skin blisters, and once in a man's eyes, the outcome was never good.

There is, I feel, a connection between what happened at Gallipoli during the First World War and what happened in Singapore. That connection is Winston Churchill. The fallout from the Commission's report on the Dardanelles campaign was far reaching and resulted in the ending of many military careers and the scarring of reputations that many never fully recovered from. Certainly Churchill himself didn't come out of the Gallipoli campaign with anything other than a crushing blow to his credibility as a politician, which I have looked at and explored in this chapter.

Move forward to 1942, 15 February to be precise, and the fall of Singapore. I have fully explored all aspects of Singapore which I have included in a subsequent chapter. In it I look at the build-up to the Japanese invasion, the final battle for the Crown Colony, and those who I felt were responsible for what has been called Britain's worst ever military disaster. Despite Churchill being the very individual who coined that particular phrase, he was the very person who determined that the debacle at Singapore did not require a public enquiry or a Commission to look into what went wrong. Remember, Churchill's own words described the loss of Singapore as Britain's worst ever military defeat, meaning that by the very nature of having said that, he must have also felt it was even worse than what had happened at Gallipoli, which was examined by a Commission. So why wasn't there something similar undertaken after Singapore? I believe that the reason is simple. After Gallipoli, Churchill experienced at first-hand how negative the fallout from a damning report could be, and it wasn't something which he was going to allow to happen again. Soon after the fall of Singapore there were calls for a public enquiry, but Churchill refused saying that it wasn't appropriate as there was still a war going on that needed to be fought and he wasn't going to waste valuable resources by tying them up with such matters.

If there had been an independent public enquiry, one as open and forthright in its findings as the one for Gallipoli, it would have been extremely embarrassing for Churchill and his government, since it would have revealed the full events of what had happened and more importantly, what hadn't been done (that should have been) for those tasked with being able to properly defend the island.

Chapter 5

The Iraq Uprising of 1920

At the end of the First World War, and with the Ottoman Empire in ruins, the bulk of the Middle East came under the control of Britain and France. But it was never going to be an easy transition.

The San Remo Conference took place at the Villa Devachan in San Remo, Italy between 19 and 26 April 1920, and was a meeting of the First World War Allied Supreme Council, which had been founded in 1917 and included members from Britain, France, America, Italy, and Japan. The main purpose of the meeting was to look at what had been three Ottoman territories in the Middle East before the start of the First World War: Syria, Palestine, and Mesopotamia.

By way of example, I will look at what during the First World War was Mesopotamia, which covered large swathes of Western Asia, but which afterwards was split into what became a large part of Iraq, the State of Kuwait, parts of Syria, the south-eastern section of Turkey, areas adjoining the Turkish and Syrian borders, as well a section of land that crossed the Iran-Iraq borders.

Not only were there now many more countries to contend with but there were also a lot of different religious and tribal factions who wanted to be included in the decision-making processes of their new country.

At the San Remo Conference, Britain had been allocated the territory of Mesopotamia under Article 22 of the Covenant of the League of Nations, which was to be categorised as a Class A mandate. This situation was not one that was agreeable or acceptable to all parties, and resulted in a nationwide revolt by the peoples of Iraq, which broke out in the summer of 1920.

It started in Baghdad with a number of demonstrations involving mainly Iraqis who were against the British occupation of their country.

There were also a number of embittered ex-Ottoman military personnel amongst the demonstrators. Over time, the demonstrations spread to different parts of the country, mainly in the middle and lower Euphrates, which were the main Shia regions of the country. One of the main protagonists was a prominent Shia leader, Sheikh Mehdi Al-Khalissi.

So strong was the anti-British feeling that Shia and Sunni communities worked together to get the British out and create an Arab-led government. A further rebellion took place in northern Iraq in 1920, when there was a Kurdish revolt led by Sheikh Mahmood Barzanji.

The Iraqi revolt had been comprehensively put down by the British by October 1920, although there was still anti-British opposition in the area as late as 1922.

One aspect of the revolt which hadn't been catered for, was the cost. The British government had spent £40 million putting down the revolt, money which so soon after the end of the First World War was money that they could ill afford. This led to the British totally rethinking how they conducted business in Iraq.

Estimates of those who were killed during the revolt, differed greatly. It is estimated that 6,000-10,000 Iraqis of all denominations were killed during the revolt, whilst about 500 British and Indian troops were also killed. But in total the British had deployed more than 100,000 men to the region during the troubles. The RAF flew a total of 4,000 hours, dropped nearly 100 tons of bombs and fired more than 180,000 rounds of ammunition whilst fighting the rebels.

During the time of the revolt, Winston Churchill was the Colonial Secretary. He was tasked with finding a way of reducing the cost of occupying the Middle East. Not an easy task as he had to somehow come up with huge budget cuts for the military, whilst ensuring Britain didn't lose her grip on the mandate it had in Iraq.

Churchill came up with what was termed as 'aerial policing', which he had first suggested to the House of Commons in March 1920, before the revolts in Iraq had even begun.

> It may be possible to effect economies during the course of the present year by holding Mesopotamia through the agency of the Air Force rather than by a military force. It has been pointed out that by your Air Force you have not

to hold long lines of communications because the distance would only be one and a half hours flight by aeroplane. It is essential in dealing with Mesopotamia to get the military expenditure down as soon as the present critical state of affairs passes away.

When trouble flared again, villages that were held by rebellious tribes were attacked by the RAF. There was one occasion when an area in the Liwa region had a number of 'recalcitrant chiefs' who refused to surrender. To try and change their minds the RAF bombed them for two days. This did the trick and resulted in most of the leaders of the offending tribes to surrender.

It is interesting to note that Churchill's idea of bombing the enemy into submission, regardless of the threat that would pose to the civilian population, caused little if no debate either in the Press or in the hallowed chambers of the House of Commons. The moral compass in relation to such events obviously wasn't in full swing in 1920. Interestingly enough, one of the squadron leaders serving in Iraq in the early 1920s was none other than Squadron Leader Arthur 'Bomber' Harris, the man who bombed Dresden during the course of the Second World War and who was accused of what by then had become known as 'area bombing'.

The bombing of Dresden was a bone of contention amongst politicians and members of high society, but not one disparaging remark against what Churchill had instigated in Iraq in the early 1920s was mooted or brought up. How quickly time changes.

Chapter 6

Black & Tans 1920

The rise of nationalism had dominated both political and everyday life throughout Ireland towards the end of the nineteenth and beginning of the twentieth centuries, as many individuals campaigned for a self-governing Ireland, within what was then the United Kingdom of Great Britain and Ireland. It was more commonly known as Home Rule.

When the First World War began, the subject of Home Rule was initially put on hold, so that there could be a united and focused fight against the Germans. But the Easter weekend in 1916, between 24 and 29 April, changed all that. What became known as the Easter Rising, an armed insurrection, was launched by Irish Republicans, for two reasons. Firstly, to end British rule throughout Ireland, and to establish an independent Irish Republic.

For the British authorities, embroiled in the brutality of the First World War, it couldn't have come at a worse time, with its military might engaged in different theatres of war stretched across Europe and beyond.

A leaflet was printed and distributed amongst the masses to curry support and favour from the Irish people.

The Provisional Government of the Irish Republic
To The People of Ireland

Irishmen and Irishwomen. In the name of God and of the dead generations from which she receives her old tradition of nationhood, Ireland through us, summons her children to her flag and strikes for her freedom.

Having organised and trained her manhood through her secret revolutionary organisation, the Irish Republican

Brotherhood, and through her open military organisations, the Irish Volunteers and the Irish Citizen Army, having patiently perfected her discipline, having resolutely waited for the right moment to reveal itself, she now seizes that moment, and supported by her exiled children in America and by her gallant allies in Europe, but relying in the first on her own strength, she strikes in full confidence of victory.

We declare the right of the people of Ireland to the ownership of Ireland, and to the unfettered control of Irish destinies, to be sovereign and indefeasible. The long usurpation of that right by a foreign people and government has not extinguished the right, nor can it ever be extinguished except by the destruction of the Irish people. In every generation the Irish people have asserted their right to national freedom and sovereignty, six times during the past three hundred years they have asserted it in arms. Standing on that fundamental right, and again asserting it in arms in the face of the world, we hereby proclaim the Irish Republic as a Sovereign Independent State, and we pledge our lives and the lives of our comrades-in-arms to the cause of its freedom, of its welfare, and of its exaltation among the nations.

The Irish Republic is entitled to, and hereby claims, the allegiance of every Irishman and Irishwoman. The Republic guarantees religious and civil liberty, equal rights and equal opportunities to all its citizens, and declares its resolve to pursue the happiness and prosperity of the whole nation and of all its parts, cherishing all the children of the nation equally, and oblivious of the differences carefully fostered by an alien government, which have divided a minority from the majority in the past.

Until our arms have brought the opportune moment for the establishment of a permanent National Government, representative of the whole people of Ireland and elected by the suffrages of all men and women, the Provisional Government, hereby constituted, will administer the civil and military affairs of the Republic in trust for the people.

We place the cause of the Irish Republic under the protection of the Most High God, whose blessing we invoke upon our arms, and we pray that no one who serves that cause will dishonour it by cowardice, inhumanity, or rapine. In this supreme hour the Irish nation must, by its valour and discipline and by the readiness of its children to sacrifice themselves for the common good, prove itself worthy of the august destiny to which it is called.

Signed on behalf of the Provisional Government,

Thomas J Clarke

Sean Mac Diarmada, Thomas MacDonagh

P H Pearse, Eamonn Ceannt,

James Connolly, Joseph Plunkett.

It was clear from the wording of the leaflet that the British government wasn't just dealing with some rag-tag bunch of daydreamers. This declaration had been well thought through and written in a considered and professional manner.

The rising began on 24 April 1916, when fighting was taking place at different locations across the Western Front, and the bombardment of Lowestoft and Yarmouth by vessels of the Imperial German Fleet was also taking place. The attack on the east coast of England was not an untimely coincidence, it was planned to coincide with the Easter Rising in Ireland, as Irish Nationalists had requested German aid.

Irish Volunteers, led by activist Padraig Pearse, a school teacher, joined together with James Connolly and his Irish Citizen Army, a paramilitary group of trade union volunteers which was Dublin-based. It was also an auxiliary of the Irish Volunteers. Between them the two groups seized some key locations in Dublin, and then proclaimed an Irish Republic. The British government reacted quickly. Realising that they were not dealing with a localised bit of rioting, they deployed thousands of troops, a gunboat and artillery units to retake the city of Dublin. But this wasn't going to be a forgone conclusion, the elements of the British army were not going to have it all their own way. The Irish Republicans had the upper hand initially, since they had chosen the location where they were going to stand and fight. As the British began to make their way through the streets and into the city centre, they came up against a dogged resistance, men and women who weren't going to give up without a fight. They managed to inflict heavy casualties on the British soldiers. But not everything went smoothly for the Irish Volunteers. Besides carrying out the naval bombardment of Lowestoft and Yarmouth, Germany had also sent a shipment of guns and ammunition to assist their Irish allies, but these were intercepted by the British. When Eoin MacNeill, a leader of the Irish Volunteers, discovered that the arms shipment had been captured by the British, he attempted to halt the rising, knowing that their efforts would be greatly affected by their loss. Some of his members received the message and some didn't, which meant that the number of fighters they had actually deployed on the streets was a lot fewer than they had originally intended.

There had been isolated incidents in other parts of Ireland and the town of Enniscorthy in the County of Wexford was taken by 600 Irish Volunteers. The British government responded by sending a force of 1,000 soldiers. In essence, once it was proven to the volunteers that their comrades in Dublin had surrendered, they did the same thing.

The British troops in Dublin had not held back in how they dealt with the situation. The Irish Republicans had put up a stiff resistance against the numerically stronger British soldiers. They fought with pride, passion and a steely determination but had no answer to being bombarded with artillery shells.

After holding the British Army at bay for six days, Padraig Pearse, one of the leaders of the Easter Rising, agreed to an unconditional surrender on Saturday, 29 April 1916.

A total of 485 people on all sides were killed in the Easter Rising, more than half of whom were civilians, but only 75 of them were what the British authorities classed as 'rebels'. A large part of the centre of Dublin was destroyed because of the artillery bombardment and subsequent fires. Between 3 and 12 May 1916, fourteen of those found guilty of offences relating to the Easter Rising were executed by the British authorities.

This wasn't the end of the matter, this was more like the beginning of it. The situation was certainly made worse because of allegations of atrocities carried out by British soldiers after the Easter Rising. An inquiry followed but very little was done to any British soldiers. The atrocities, and the 'tepid' inquiry that followed, went a long way to seeing the formation of Sinn Fein, and the troubles that followed.

In January 1919, just two months after the end of the signing of the Armistice, Winston Churchill was made Secretary of State for War, as well as Secretary of State for Air. If he imagined he was going to be in for an easy time, now that the Armistice had been signed, he was wrong. Within only a matter of days of him being sworn into office, the Irish War of Independence began on 21 January 1919, with what has become known as the Soloheadbeg Ambush in County Tipperary, when a number of members of the 3rd Tipperary Brigade, Irish Republican Army, carried out an unauthorised ambush which resulted in the deaths of two members of the Royal Ulster Constabulary, Constables Patrick O'Connell and James McDonnell, along with the theft of a large amount of gelignite, which they were escorting at the time. The murder of the two members of the Royal Irish Constabulary took place on the same day as Sinn Fein assembled in Dublin, and formed the First Dail, or Parliament, and officially announced the Irish Declaration of Independence. It is worth noting at this stage that although the Armistice had been signed and the fighting had stopped, Britain was still at war with Germany until 28 June 1919, when the Treaty of Versailles was signed, officially ending the war between Britain and Germany.

Somewhat fortunately for the Prime Minister David Lloyd George, Churchill, in his capacity as Secretary of State for War and in charge of demobilising the wartime British army had persuaded him to keep 1 million men under conscription, to be used mainly as an Army of Occupation on the Rhine in Germany. With the troubles in Ireland having flared up as well, it turned out to be a good decision.

Matters started to develop reasonably quickly after this. On 23 February 1919, at a meeting of the 3rd Tipperary Brigade, held at Nodstown, Tipperary, a proclamation was issued by the IRA and signed by their commanding officer, Seamus Robinson, which ordered all British soldiers and local police officers out of South Tipperary. Those who failed to heed the order did so at the risk of losing their lives.

It became apparent that not everyone was in agreement with the proclamation: the leadership of the Irish Volunteers in Dublin refused to sanction it and instructed that it not be displayed publicly – which it was.

With a continuous number of shootings, attacks, woundings and killings being carried out, and no sign of it coming to an end, Winston Churchill took the decision to deploy the paramilitary Black and Tans – a force of temporary constables – to Ireland on 25 March 1920. Their job was to support the full-time members of the Royal Irish Constabulary in their fight with the Irish Republican Army (IRA) and to help maintain law and order amongst the civilian population. The Black and Tans infamy arose out of their attacks on civilians and their homes.

Although their proper title was Royal Irish Constabulary Special Reserve, they acquired the nickname because of the colours of their uniforms.

Besides being the person responsible for the Black and Tans' deployment to Ireland, Churchill had also been responsible for their recruitment, which had begun in Great Britain in the final months of 1919. With tens of thousands of men having been demobbed following the signing of the Armistice, there were plenty of men willing to sign up, even though the British government had openly advertised the job as being for men who were willing to 'face a rough and dangerous task'. For men who had already served in the trenches of the First World War, and seen death and destruction on a daily basis, those words didn't hold any fears or concerns. Most who joined were First World War veterans who had returned home after the war, been demobilised and who could not find work.

By sending in the Black and Tans, it would appear that Winston Churchill and the British government were taken by surprise by the events in Ireland, which if true, is unbelievable. It doesn't seem possible after everything that had gone on beforehand. The Easter Rising of 1916 was a massive indicator of the feeling of the Irish people and the Irish General Election of 1918 saw Sinn Fein win 73 out of the 105 seats available, an even bigger indicator of how high anti-British feeling was in Ireland. Yet Lloyd George and Churchill still didn't seem to understand the severity of the situation they were dealing with. It was if they felt the opposition they were dealing with was just an unintelligent group of thugs and a passing phase. The public reaction after the leaders of the

Easter Rising in 1916 were executed should have been a strong indicator of how the future might be where Ireland was concerned.

What Churchill and Lloyd George also didn't seem to grasp was the long-term damage sending in the Black and Tans into Ireland was going to cause. Things were never going to be resolved by the use of violence from the state against a civilian population, all that achieved was to ensure the hatred and distrust that Irish people had for the British remained and became a family as well as a group dilemma.

'Knock one man down, and his son will return in the next generation to even the score,' but this wasn't a scenario that was recognised by either Churchill or Lloyd George.

All Churchill had to do to properly visualise the depth of the problem he was encountering, was to think about how he would have felt if England, as a sovereign nation, was being ruled by another country. Once he understood how that felt, he might then have had the answer on how best to resolve the situation.

By November 1921, 9,500 men had been recruited into the Black and Tans, and whether Churchill knew or not, he had created a beast. Many more men enlisted than had been anticipated, meaning there was a shortage of Royal Irish Constabulary uniforms to put them in, so instead they were issued khaki-coloured army trousers and blue British police tunics, caps and belts. This concoction of uniform made them look neither like members of the Royal Irish Constabulary nor the British army.

All new recruits to the Black and Tans underwent three months of basic training, before being allocated to an RIC barracks, either in Munster, County Dublin, or Connaught. Churchill and the British government raised another unit also destined for Ireland. Known as the Auxiliaries or the 'Auxies' it was made up of ex-British army officers. The difference between the two units was that the Black and Tans were in place to back up the Royal Irish Constabulary in their normal, run of the mill, day-to-day duties, and the fight against the IRA, whilst the Auxiliaries were offensive mobile units, whose job it was to actively locate and take out units of the IRA. So as to be effective in their task, they were heavily armed with sufficient fire power to be able to deal with the various scenarios in which they might find themselves.

From an historical point of view it would appear that there is a certain amount of confusion concerning the Black and Tans, in that their reputation for being cold-blooded, ruthless killers might have been unfairly enhanced by being attributed with having carried out atrocities that they hadn't committed, but which had actually been carried out by the Auxiliaries.

The difference between then and now is that no matter whatever scrutiny police officers find themselves under, it is far greater now than it was 100 years previously. Then, they appear have been able to do exactly what they wanted, with little or no official comeback, and with support from the British government, especially if 'police' action was in response to an IRA attack.

Reading about what the Black and Tans were responsible for, especially in the second half of 1920, after they had arrived in Ireland, makes for uncomfortable reading, especially when taking into account that they were brought into existence and put in place by Winston Churchill and the British government, then given almost free rein to do exactly what it was they wanted to do. It wasn't uncommon for the Black and Tans to take revenge on civilian populations if their own men were killed in IRA attacks. It wasn't just people they took their revenge on, it was their properties as well. July 1920 saw them set fire to and sack the County Galway town of Tuam and the County Meath town of Trim (situated as it is on the banks of the River Boyne, with its Norman castle). The same fate befell the town of Balbriggan, the village of Knockcroghery, and the towns of Thurles and Templemore.

In November 1920, the IRA abducted and murdered two members of the RIC from Tralee. The Black and Tans response was brutal. No food was allowed into the town for a week, all businesses were closed, and three members of the public were shot dead.

On the evening of 11 December 1920, six members of the IRA carried out an attack on two military lorries that had left the Victoria Barracks in Cork, carrying members of the Auxiliary who were going out on patrol. By means of subterfuge, they managed to stop the first lorry soon after it had left the barracks, before beginning their attack with small-arms fire and grenades. Twelve of the Auxiliaries were wounded, one of whom died a short while later. This provoked one of the bloodiest reprisals that the Auxiliaries had ever carried out.

Later the same evening, a number of Auxiliaries and Black and Tans, along with British soldiers, made their way in the centre of Cork, and took their revenge by setting fire to the city centre. By the following morning an estimated 300 residential homes, 40 businesses, the Carnegie Library and the City Hall, had all been set on fire and ruined, resulting in thousands of people being left homeless. The cost of the damage was estimated to be in the region of £3 million, the equivalent of £145 million in today's value.

In the aftermath of the attack, firemen testified to the authorities that they had been prevented on more than one occasion from trying to put out the fires by British forces, and had even experienced having their fire hoses cut.

An event on this scale could simply not go unnoticed. Irish nationalists requested an independent and impartial inquiry into the events of 11/12 December, but remarkably their request was rejected by Sir Hamar Greenwood, the Chief Secretary for Ireland. He went even further, by claiming that British forces had not set Cork on fire, the IRA had. Despite the incredulous response by the government, the British military launched its own inquiry. The 'Strickland Report' so named after its Chairman, General Strickland, was completed in February 1921, and it pointed the finger of blame for the events of 11/12 December 1920 at the members of 'K' Company, the Auxiliaries, who were based at the city's Victoria Barracks. It was further claimed that the destruction of Cork was in reprisal for the IRA attack on the Auxiliaries at Dillon's Cross. Despite these findings, the government refused to publish Strickland's report.

In January 1921, a report on the situation in Ireland was produced by the British Labour Commission. It was extremely critical of the British government's security policy in Ireland. The report particularly mentioned the Black and Tans and its relationship with the government, and how the latter failed to have any control, willingly or otherwise over the former. It also claimed that since the end of December 1920, the British government had allowed what the report referred to as 'official reprisals' in Ireland. This usually meant attacking and burning the homes of known IRA members and others who were sympathetic to their cause. The sanctioned 'official reprisals' actually helped prevent the Black and Tans from acting on their own initiative, especially in the aftermath of an IRA attack on one of their barracks or stations, or if one of their own men were killed.

At that time, Winston Churchill was the Secretary of War, a position in the Cabinet of the British government; he headed the War Office. Of the three senior individuals he would have had working for him, one would have been a military secretary of the rank of general. Another would have been a Parliamentary Under-Secretary of State for War, and a Parliamentary Private Secretary, so it is inconceivable that Winston Churchill would not have had some knowledge of what the Black and Tans and the Auxiliaries were doing in Ireland. It is also inconceivable that these two organisations would have acted unilaterally and independent of the government's wishes and political priorities in Ireland.

What was truly staggering about Winston Churchill and the British government was their total inability to realise the damage that the Black and Tans were doing to them politically and in the minds of the public. Their continued penchant for extreme violence against the civilian population simply made the IRA stronger and more appealing to a large percentage of the Irish population. It was clear that the situation in Ireland had to be resolved and couldn't be allowed to continue.

The Conservative MP of for Ripon, Edward Wood, who would later go on to become Lord Halifax, urged the British government to make an offer to the Irish. Other far-sighted Conservatives urged a similar approach. Ireland had become a no-win situation for Churchill and the government but the only ones who couldn't seem to grasp the fact was them.

In the House of Lords, on 16 February 1921, Sir Hamar Greenwood, Chief Secretary for Ireland, was heckled by Irish Nationalists for refusing to publish General Strickland's report on the destruction caused in the city of Cork.

The *Times* newspaper dated 17 February 1921, said the prime minister's speech earlier in the week was 'nothing more than a confession of the failure of his Irish administration'.

Regarding the government's decision not to publish the Strickland report, the article added:

> While the government has already said enough about events in Cork to confirm the worst suspicions, it has failed significantly to show the candour which could alone have disposed of the charge that it dare not publish the full truth. Now however, there is no longer room for doubt that the Irish administration must bear the stain of lasting disgrace, which

cannot fail of reaction upon the good repute of England. The authors of the present policy of the Irish administration are directly to blame for the connivance which rendered the burnings in Cork possible.

The list of those critical of the actions of the Black and Tans just kept on growing. Lionel Curtis, a professor and author, wrote in *The Round Table: The Commonwealth Journal of Affairs,* an international relations journal, 'If the British Commonwealth can only be preserved by such means, it would become a negation of the principle for which it has stood.'

King George V was most definitely not amused at the actions of the Black and Tans, nor were some senior Anglican Bishops, MPs from different parties, Oswald Mosely, Jan Smuts, who at the time was the prime minister of South Africa, the Trades' Union Congress, along with elements of the national Press. Mahatma Gandhi, the leader of the Indian Independence movement against British colonial rule, said of the offer of peace by the British Government, 'It is not the fear of losing more lives that has compelled a reluctant offer from England, but it is the shame of any further imposition of agony upon a people that loves liberty above everything else ...'

Roughly 7,000 men signed up to serve with the Black and Tans in Ireland between 1920 and 1922. Along with their full-time colleagues in the RIC they were disbanded in 1922, and collectively some 600 of them were wounded and a further 404 of them were killed, or died as a result of their service in Ireland. What the breakdown is of RIC, Auxiliaries or Black and Tans amongst the casualty figures is not known.

The captain of 'K' Company Auxiliary was Charles Schultz, who during the First World War, had served with the British army. In the aftermath of the attack he wrote two letters home to England, one to his mother and the other to his girlfriend. The letter to his mother included, 'Many who had witnessed scenes in France and Flanders, say that nothing they had experienced was comparable with the punishment meted out in Cork.' The letter to his girlfriend included, 'Sweet revenge'.

For their part in the burning and looting of Cork city, 'K' Company was disbanded on 31 March 1921.

It was interesting to note that in the immediate aftermath of the completion of the Strickland report, not only was there a noticeable absence of any comment from Winston Churchill, but on 13 February 1921, he transferred from being the Secretary of State for Air and War, to become the Secretary of State for the Colonies, a position he would retain until 19 October 1921.

The Anglo-Irish Treaty, which saw the end of the Irish War of Independence, was signed at 10 Downing Street, on 6 December 1922. One of the signatures on the typed agreement is that of Winston Churchill, which as the man who was responsible for the recruitment and the sending of the Black and Tans to Ireland to help the RIC fight against the IRA, was tinged with a certain amount of irony. Some would see Churchill's part in a positive way, saying that he saw the opportunity for peace and dialogue between Britain and Irish Republicans and pushed it forward. Some wouldn't necessarily agree with that assessment, the other option being that he finally realised that to persevere with his tactic of sending in the Black and Tans, along with the Auxiliaries, and letting them behave in the manner in which they did, resulting in ever-increasing death and destruction, had started to prove counter-productive and had created a negative image of both the British government and Winston Churchill, which in his case was not in keeping with his long-term personal political aims.

The commanding officer of the first Black and Tan recruits was Lieutenant Colonel Gerald Smyth, who had fought in the First World War with the Royal Engineers and had been mentioned in despatches seven times, been badly wounded but survived, and was a man known for his Unionist sympathies.

On 19 June 1920, he allegedly made a speech to the ranks of the Listowel Royal Irish Constabulary. I have seen two versions of this speech and I have no idea which one of them is correct, or whether either of them is.

> Should the order 'Hands Up' not be immediately obeyed, shoot and shoot with effect. If the persons approaching a patrol carry their hands in their pockets, or are in any way suspicious looking, shoot them down. You may make mistakes occasionally and innocent persons may be shot, but that cannot be helped, and you are bound to get the right parties some time.

The more you shoot, the better I will like you, and I assure you no policeman will get into trouble for shooting any man ... hunger-strikers will be allowed to die in jail, the more the merrier. Some of them have died already and a damn bad job they were not all allowed to die.

As a matter of fact, some of them have already been dealt with in a manner their friends will never hear about. An emigrant ship left an Irish port for a foreign port lately with lots of Sinn Feiners on board, I assure you men it will never land. That is nearly all I have to say to you. General Tudor and myself want your assistance in carrying out this scheme and wiping out Sinn Fein. Any man who is prepared to be a hindrance rather than a help to us, had better leave the job at once.

The second version of Smyth's speech, had the following piece at the beginning of the speech:

Police and military will patrol the country roads at least five nights a week. They are not to confine themselves to the main roads, but make across the country, lie in ambush, take cover behind fences near roads, and when civilians are seen approaching, shout: 'Hands up!'

At the end of the second line in the second paragraph, the following was included in the second version:

'and I will guarantee that your names will not be given at the inquest.'

One of those present at the speech was Constable Jeremiah Mee, who was so disgusted by what he had heard Smyth say that he challenged him directly, saying, 'By your accent I take it you are an Englishman and, in your ignorance, forget that you are addressing Irishmen.'

Mee then removed his uniform, and along with his rifle laid it on a table, calling Smyth a murderer as he did so. Smyth ordered Mee's immediate arrest, but none of his colleagues would do so. Mee and thirteen others resigned on the spot and left. This incident became known as the 'Listowel Mutiny'.

Although he wasn't aware at the time, Smyth would pay dearly for his comments. Smyth's speech to the RIC constables at Listowel marked him for attention from the IRA. He subsequently returned to Cork and took up lodgings at the prestigious Cork & County Club, an Anglo-Irish social club. On the evening of 17 July 1920, he was relaxing in the smoking room when a six-man IRA team led by Daniel O'Donovan entered and allegedly said to him, 'Colonel, were not your orders to shoot on sight? Well you are in sight now, so prepare.'

Colonel Smyth jumped to his feet before being riddled with bullets by the IRA men. He was shot twice in the head, once through the heart and twice through the chest. The colonel staggered a few feet where he dropped dead.

Lieutenant Colonel Gerald Smyth was buried at Banbridge, County Down on 20 July 1920. His funeral was followed by three days of reprisals against local Roman Catholic homes and businesses. One Protestant man was shot by the RIC and killed, and three Irish nationalists were convicted of firearms offences.

Smyth's brother, George Osbert Smyth, who was a member of the 'Cairo Gang', a group of British intelligence officers, also served in Ireland, and was stationed in Dublin. His job was to spy on and eliminate leading figures within the IRA. He was shot dead in October 1920 at a house in Drumcondra, where he had gone to carry out the arrest of IRA members.

There are obvious questions to be asked in relation to Winston Churchill and his connection to, and knowledge of, the Black and Tans and the atrocities and killings they carried out. Their remit was to assist the RIC in their dealings with the IRA, but what were their rules of engagement, and who gave them their instructions from the British government? One would assume that it was somebody who worked within the War Office, the very department that was headed by the Secretary of State for War, Winston Churchill.

When it was 'discovered' what the Black and Tans were doing, why did the War Office not act? Why did it take such eminent individuals as King George V, and reports such as the one submitted by General Strickland (which the government refused to publish), before they acted?

The following are questions asked in the House of Commons in relation to the Black and Tans. On 24 February 1921, Captain Coote asked the Chief Secretary for Ireland whether any code of discipline had been issued for the guidance of the force known as the Black and Tans; if so, by whom was it issued and at what date; and how long elapsed between the employment of any portion of this force and the issue of such a code?

Sir H. Greenwood provided the somewhat remarkable, if not comical, response that the Royal Irish Constabulary Disciplinary Code applied, and had applied at all times, and to all branches of the force. On the balance of probabilities that just a small percentage of allegations of damage, assault and murder, were factual, the obvious question that is then thrown up, is why wasn't the disciplinary code utilised a lot more against officers who were involved in some of the high-profile incidents? I can answer the one about why no one was disciplined with the sacking and burning of Cork. The British government claimed it was the IRA (and not British soldiers), who carried it out.

Sir H. Greenwood was a busy man on 24 February 1921, having to field numerous questions on the topic of the Black and Tans.

One of the questions put to him was by a Mr Mosley, who asked the Chief Secretary for Ireland whether he had made any enquiries into the affidavit sworn by Joseph Murphy from Dublin, in which he claimed he received information from his brother, James Murphy, when dying of bullet wounds in hospital. He asked Greenwood if he was aware that the affidavit stated that James Murphy was arrested, searched in Dublin Castle, acquitted of any crime against the law, and returned to his home under escort for the purpose of his safety, as it was after curfew hour, and further stated that on the way home he and his companion were instructed by the escort to get out of the lorry they were in, and shot. They were left for dead on a piece of waste ground. Could he produce any evidence in relation to this affidavit, sworn before Cecil George Stapleton, a commissioner of oaths?

Sir H. Greenwood informed Mr Mosley that two members of the Auxiliary Division and one other person had been arrested and would be charged with the murder of James Murphy.

In any other circumstances some of the actions carried out by the Black and Tans and the Auxiliaries would have undoubtedly been deemed to have constituted war crimes and dealt with accordingly. How far up the chain of command that would have gone, is debateable, but it could have resulted in certain politicians facing criminal charges.

Chapter 7

Invasion of Norway 1940

Norway was a neutral country at the outbreak of the Second World War, but unbeknown to the governments of both Norway and Britain, Germany had been planning an invasion of Norway since December 1939, which was given the operational code name of *Weserubung*. There were two reasons behind this: firstly, Germany moved her merchant vessels through Norwegian waters, bringing much-needed iron ore to her own ports, but her concern was also that Britain would either work out what she was doing, or might decide to invade Norway herself, to gain control of the iron ore deposits in neighbouring Sweden. At the beginning of the war, Germany was already importing 10 million tons of iron ore from Sweden.

On 19 September 1939, Winston Churchill, the newly appointed First Lord of the Admiralty, told the government Cabinet members, including Chamberlain, that they had to do something to prevent the iron ore leaving Narvik from reaching Germany. His colleagues listened but nothing came of the meeting in relation to Norway. Not put off by the Cabinet's apparent reluctance to do anything over Narvik, ten days later Churchill tried again. This time he put forward the suggestion that they should mine the approaches to the port of Narvik, if there was any indication of a continuation of iron ore shipments leaving from there, which to the best of his knowledge had not taken place since the beginning of the war. Despite his protestations, the Cabinet did not approve his recommendation stating that they did not wish to take such a course of action, as it would breach Norway's neutrality.

Let me clear up any confusion concerning iron ore and Norway and Sweden. As I have already said in the above paragraph, Germany imported her iron ore from Sweden, but during the winter months, the

Swedish port of Lulea, which was her first choice to ship the ore from, was entirely frozen over and inaccessible to shipping. During these months the ore was moved by train to the Norwegian port of Narvik, and shipped from there.

Control of Norway and her coastline would also help the Germans in the battle for the control of the North Sea and provide easier passage for her ships and submarines into the Atlantic.

On 16 February 1940, just five months into the war, an incident took place which placed enormous pressure on that status. It became known as the *Altmark* incident. The *Altmark* was a German auxiliary ship, who in the early months of the war, had acted as a support vessel for the mighty German cruiser, the *Admiral Graf Spee* which during the same period of time had been attacking Allied merchant vessels in the South Atlantic. The *Altmark* was sailing through Norwegian waters with a Norwegian naval escort, and flying a German national flag rather than a Nazi one. Her cargo that day was neither iron ore or oil, but 299 Allied prisoners of war who had been taken from some of the Allied merchant vessels previously attacked by the *Admiral Graf Spee.*

When the *Altmark* entered the Jossingfjorden she was boarded by British naval personnel from HMS *Cossack.* During the boarding, seven crew members of the *Altmark* were killed, whilst all of the 299 prisoners were safely rescued. At no time did the three Norwegian naval vessels who were escorting the *Altmark* through Norwegian waters, intervene in the British attack. As might be expected, the outcome of the incident led to complaints and protests by all three sides. What the incident did do was to galvanise the German resolve, and increased her desire to carry out her invasion of Norway as soon as possible.

The Allies were concerned that an Allied occupation of either Norway or Sweden could well end up being counter-productive, and might result in both countries entering the war on the side of Germany. Churchill had long been in favour of taking some kind of action in Scandinavia, because he wanted the countries in that region to side with Britain and her Allies, and not Germany. The issue over Norway between Germany and Britain really did become like a game of cat and mouse, with one side trying to guess what the other side may or may not do. Would they invade or wouldn't they? Was it better to have them on our side, or to remain neutral?

Churchill in typical pose outside Downing Street. (*Public domain*)

'Allies' sculpture of Roosevelt and Churchill in New Bond Street, London. (© *chrisdorney/Adobe Stock*)

Sculpture of Churchill in the village of Westerhall, Kent. (*Ross Burgess, CC BY-SA 3.0*)

At the Sidney Street siege, January 1911. (*Public domain*)

Churchill, who was Home Secretary at the time, at the Sidney Street siege. (*Public domain*)

Churchill's funeral procession. (*Public domain*)

Campaigning for the General
Election 1945. (*Public domain*)

Above left: Churchill - With Charles de Gaulle and others. (*Public domain*)

Above right: Churchill, then First Lord of the Admiralty, pictured in London, 1912. (*Public domain*)

Statue of Churchill in Parliament Square. (© *Sergii Figurnyi/Adobe Stock*)

Churchill, Roosevelt and Stalin at the Yalta Conference, February 1945. (*Public domain*)

With his then fiancée Clementine in 1908. (*Public domain*)

Above: Churchill addressing the public in Whitehall on VE Day. (*Public domain*)

Left: Churchill's famous 'V for Victory' sign, taken May 1943. (*Public domain*)

Inspecting the ruined Coventry Cathedral after the german bombing in November 1940. (*Public domain*)

With Blackie, the mascot of HMS Prince of Wales, August 1941. (*Public domain*)

Young Churchill, pictured in 1895 in the military uniform of the Fourth Queen's Own Hussars. (*Public domain*)

Firing a Thompson Sub-machine gun alongside General Dwight D. Eisenhower, March 1944. (*Public domain*)

Enter Winston Churchill fully into the equation. On 3 September 1940, the then British Prime Minister, Neville Chamberlain, appointed Churchill as First Lord of the Admiralty. By the time of the problems of what to do with Norway had been fully explored, Britain was not in a good place militarily. The war in Europe was not going well at all. It is quite possible that because of her other military commitments, such as the invasion of Poland, that Germany did not invade Norway sooner than she actually did.

The feasibility study on the invasion of Norway by Hitler's military intelligence branch had commenced on 14 December 1939, but the attack on the *Altmark* moved proceedings ahead at a quicker pace than would have otherwise been. After General von Falkenhorst, the man who had been tasked with carrying out the invasion of Norway reported that his plans were complete, Hitler ordered, on 1 March 1940, that all such preparations for an invasion of Norway should begin. On 1 April, and with everything finally in place, Hitler ordered that the attack on Norway should begin on 9 April. Thankfully British intelligence had discovered Germany's intentions, and plans were put in place for selected army units to be put on standby in Scotland, in case the Germans moved to invade Norway.

With subsequent German shipping movements indicating that an attack on Norway was imminent, on 7 April 1940 the Royal Air Force carried out an attack on the German vessels, but without any success. The same day, the Home Fleet set off from Scapa Flow, to commence Operation Wilfred, which was the laying of mines off Norway and specifically across the mouth of the port at Narvik.

The British actions failed to prevent the German invasion of Norway from going ahead, which had included German troops being landed at the Norwegian ports of Oslo, Kristiansand, Trondheim, Bergen and Narvik. Part of Germany's success was down to the inclement weather which prevailed at the time of the invasion, not only as cover, but in slowing down the journey of the British vessels of the Home Fleet. When the first of the German soldiers were landing the Royal Navy were still many miles away from the Norwegian coast. Such was the speed and tenacity of the attack that the Norwegians were taken totally by surprise, and at first were not aware of what was actually taking place. Once they had taken stock of the situation, they realised their only sensible option was to surrender.

When the British authorities became aware of the full extent of the German invasion, which resulted in more than 100,000 men, as well as Panzer and artillery units landing along the Norwegian coast they immediately began to make preparations for a counter invasion, but there was disagreement on the best way to achieve it. Senior British Army officers preferred to conduct landings at Trondheim, whilst others, including Winston Churchill, preferred landings at Narvik, which also allowed for the slightly misplaced propaganda opportunity of having reclaimed the town. In the end troops were landed at both locations.

This was yet another example of Churchill, in his capacity as a politician, trying to overrule senior military personnel who were more knowledgeable and experienced in such matters. This was one of Churchill's less endearing traits. Once he got an idea in his head about the way a military option should be undertaken, being flexible in his approach wasn't something which he found at all easy. What was quite surprising with Churchill was that he didn't seem to learn from his previous experiences, Gallipoli being the prime example. I appreciate that men are killed in war, but when military operations are pushed ahead against the best advice available, and they go wrong, men die when they needn't have, nor shouldn't have. Knowing that men had died because an operation went ahead against advice, would haunt most men for the rest of their lives.

On 8 April 1940, the waters approaching the northern Norwegian port of Narvik, were mined by vessels of the Royal Navy. This was not a decision that the British and French governments had taken lightly, as Norway was a neutral country. The need to take such drastic action was because this was the route that iron ore left Sweden on its way to Germany. On 9 April 1940, Germany invaded Norway, which, although selected army units were on standby for such an event, still came as a surprise as intelligence services had not determined which date the invasion might be. This was a situation that did not bode well with the British military or politicians.

Britain's next total surprise came just four weeks later on 2 May 1940. After only four weeks of fighting the Germans in Norway, Neville Chamberlain announced in the House of Commons, that British forces in Norway were being withdrawn. This was the final nail in Chamberlain's coffin and he stepped down and Churchill, to everybody's surprise, possibly even including himself, became prime minister.

At Churchill's request, a hastily gathered force of men was put together to return to Norway in an effort to try and prevent further Norwegian ports from being captured by the Germans. It was a multinational group, pulled together from Poland, France and Britain. The French soldiers were from their nation's elite mountain unit.

The shocking thing about the Allies and their involvement in Norway, was there were definite similarities between actions taken there and what happened at Gallipoli during the First World War. Once again it was that man Churchill who was at the helm of pushing through 'the attack', but it quickly became apparent that once again, he was simply out of his depth, despite some strong characters amongst the group of senior military men who were advising him. But although what history has recorded as the Norwegian Campaign was deemed a disaster for Britain and her Allies, it did result in the evacuation of the Norwegian royal family and the saving of the nation's gold reserve.

Allied attempts at ending the German occupation of Norway commenced with the First and Second Battles of Narvik, which took place on 10 April 1940. The first battle commenced at 4.30am, when the Royal Navy destroyers HMS *Hardy, Havock, Hotspur, Hostile,* and *Hunter*, arrived undetected due to combination of fog and snow, outside the harbour at Narvik, with their main objective being to guard the entrance. On their arrival they discovered five German destroyers, which they chose to engage. To that extent the battle was a success as the British managed to sink two destroyers, and severely damaged a third. They also sank a further six supply vessels that were also at anchor within the harbour. Where things went wrong for the British was that they made one too many passes of the German vessels, and on the third one the British vessels under the command of Captain Warburton-Lee were attacked by a number of German destroyers, which resulted in HMS *Hardy, Hunter* and *Hotspur* all being severely damaged.

The Second Battle of Narvik saw the British do much better. The Germans had one of their submarines sunk by an aircraft of the RAF, and all the remaining German vessels at Narvik, having run out of fuel and ammunition, abandoned their ships and scuttled them.

Operation Alphabet, the Allied decision to retreat from Norway, was initiated on 24 May 1940, and began on 28 May. This included British, French and Polish troops. The evacuation was completed by 8 June 1940 and all remaining Norwegian troops surrendered to the Germans on 10 June 1940.

The irony of the Norway campaign was that it was one of the events in the early months of the Second World War which resulted in the end of Chamberlain's term as the British prime minister, and the man who took over from him was of course Winston Churchill, who as the First Lord of the Admiralty, had been the main architect of the Norway campaign, and as such was responsible for many of the mistakes that were made.

Chapter 8

SS Lancastria 1940

The SS *Lancastria* was sunk off St Nazaire, on the north-west coastline of France, on Monday, 17 June 1940, during Operation Ariel, which had begun two days earlier. It has gone down in maritime history as the largest loss of life in the sinking of any British ship throughout history, and Winston Churchill ordered that news of the sinking should be kept secret from the British public.

What is not known is exactly how many people lost their lives when the *Lancastria* sank. Before the war she was the Cunard ocean-going liner RMS *Lancastria* and could carry a maximum of 2,200 passengers with a crew of 375. On the day she sank it has been estimated that there were between 4,000 and 9,000 mainly British military personnel on board, although the exact number of those who were lost will never be known.

I will be writing about the entire story of the loss of the SS *Lancastria* in a separate book, but on these pages I will just be writing about Winston Churchill's subsequent cover-up of that day's event.

Churchill ordered the cover-up, he said, to help keep up the nation's morale as they had already had to deal with enough bad news so far in the war. What he was referring to was the first ten months of the war, during which time there had been nothing but disaster after disaster for the Allies.

After the Norway campaign, a huge debate was held in the House of Commons between 7 and 9 May 1940, which looked at a number of British defeats that culminated in what was seen by many as the debacle of Norway. The debate brought to a head the widespread dissatisfaction with the overall conduct of the war by Chamberlain's Conservative-dominated government. So intense was the debate that it had resulted in the resignation of Neville Chamberlain on 10 May 1940 and the replacement of his war ministry.

The Norway campaign had taken place whilst the British Expeditionary Force was being pushed back through Belgium and France, as the Germans swept all before them, and which resulted in the evacuation of hundreds of thousands of British and Allied soldiers on the beaches of Dunkirk.

I believe Churchill learnt a never-to-be-forgotten lesson with the downfall of Neville Chamberlain. He saw at first hand, how not doing well in a war was not a good strategy for one's longevity in politics, especially if you were the prime minister.

Now returning to the subject of this chapter, the SS *Lancastria*, I believe the real reason Winston Churchill wanted to keep the sinking of the *Lancastria* a secret and away from the ears of the nation, wasn't to prevent the public's morale from being negatively affected, but to keep his job. Remember, the evacuations at Dunkirk had only concluded on 4 June 1940, just ten days before the *Lancastria* was attacked and sunk, and when they began Operation Dynamo, its outcome was far from certain. I believe Churchill was concerned that if news of the sinking of the *Lancastria* leaked out, then his tenure as prime minister would be an extremely short one indeed. Having witnessed how swiftly the great political tide had turned against Chamberlain after the two-day debate in early May 1940, he didn't want the same thing to happen to him. After all, he had spent a long time trying to get to the top of the tree in politics, and at the ripe old age of 65 he wasn't about to give it up so quickly or easily. Churchill wasn't going to allow the sinking of the *Lancastria*, tragic though it undoubtedly was, to end his time as prime minister. That, I would suggest, was never going to happen.

Chapter 9

Sinking of the French Fleet 1940

In April 1940, the French had considered signing an armistice with Germany, which would have taken all their military personnel out of the war, but it would have also put all their military hardware in the hands of the Germans, who would have then undoubtedly used it against Britain and her allies. Winston Churchill worked his magic and convinced the French not to do so.

The evacuations at Dunkirk at the end of May 1940 had seen troops from Belgium, Britain and France make good their escape to the UK, but only by the skin of their teeth, and so managing to keep their nations' soldiers in the war. But no sooner had the immediate euphoria of Dunkirk subsided, than the French informed Churchill that they wanted to sign a separate armistice with Germany. He was not at all amused.

America was yet to enter the war at this stage, in fact she was still some eighteen months away from doing so. For the UK to lose one of her main Allies so early in the fight would be a devastating blow.

The main concern for Churchill was if France did capitulate, what would become of her navy and all her ships. Regardless of what did or did happen with France, there was no way he was going to allow any of those vessels to fall into the hands of the Germans. At the outbreak of the Second World War, the French navy, or the *Marine Nationale,* was the fourth strongest navy in the world, so to have such ships used against them would have done Britain absolutely no good at all.

Although the French army had done its best to stave off the German onslaught, by the first week of June 1940 they were already a spent force. But remarkably the French navy was still relatively intact. French Admiral Francois Darlan, the man in charge of France's navy, had categorically assured Churchill that the entire fleet would be scuttled before it was either surrendered or captured by the Germans. But Churchill was not totally convinced, and his concern was the actual ships themselves. He was fairly happy that the French would not just simply hand their fleet over to the Germans. His concern was that if the Germans decided that they were going to take the ships, all they had to do was put their own men on board, get them up to speed and then turn on the British. That was something that Churchill was not prepared to let happen.

Time was running out and Churchill knew it. All he had to do was to convince others within the War Cabinet of the same. On 17 June 1940, the ante went up somewhat, when France pressed for peace with Germany. Churchill tried to persuade the War Cabinet to let him attack the French fleet, rather than run the risk of allowing it to fall into the hands of the Germans after they had surrendered. The War Cabinet refused. They just could not seem to see the bigger picture. Their thought process was somewhat restrictive and they seemed more obsessed with playing by Queensberry rules rather than doing whatever it was that needed doing for the safety of the nation and its people. France and Germany signed their armistice on 24 June 1940, this really did make it somewhat of a guessing game for Churchill and the War Cabinet. A case of 'will they won't they' if ever there was one.

The War Cabinet were concerned that the attack might result in the loss of some of their own troops and one or more of their ships. Yes, there was the possibility of both of those eventualities. Despite France's decision to 'surrender' she was still Britain's ally.

After the signing of the armistice, remarkably Hitler allowed France to keep all her naval vessels. He didn't want the French to have an excuse to come back into the war, especially on the side of Great Britain, so if keeping her ships helped keep the status quo, then that was fine with him. Churchill wasn't having any of it. He had seen Hitler sign many similar deals in the past only to then renege on them further down the line. He didn't trust him.

Churchill must have had a very persuasive manner, because it was the War Cabinet who buckled first on 1 July 1940, when they changed their minds and gave Churchill permission to sink the French fleet if they failed to surrender. Churchill reacted immediately and ordered Force H, who were based at Gibraltar, to surround the Algerian port of Mers-el-Kebir, near Oran, where the French fleet was at anchor and under the command of Admiral Marcel Gensoul. The French vessels included the battlecruisers *Dunkerque* and *Strasbourg,* the battleships *Provence* and *Bretagne,* and several destroyers.

Churchill had told his naval commander, Admiral Sir James Somerville, to pass on a clear and precise message to their French counterparts: 'Sail your ships to Britain or America or scuttle your ships within the next six hours or they will be destroyed.' Initially the French were not happy with such an ultimatum and refused to engage in any negotiations with the British. But two hours later the French showed the British an order they had been given by Admiral Darlan which instructed them to sail their ships to America if the Germans showed the slightest sign of breaking the terms of their armistice and tried to take command of the French fleet.

Possibly unbeknown to the French naval commanders, a message had been intercepted by the British, ordering reinforcements to urgently make their way to Oran in Algeria. The message had been sent by the Vichy government. Enough was enough as far as Churchill was concerned. The games were over. He had 'asked nicely' once, he wasn't going to do it again. He gave his commanders the order to attack, and Operation Catapult was put into place. An hour and a half later they did just that. The British, under the command of Admiral Somerville, opened fire on their French counterparts, and within ten minutes 1,297 French sailors had been killed. One battleship was destroyed and five other ships were damaged.

The French were understandably extremely angry about the events at Oran. As for Churchill, he received nothing but praise for his decisive actions, although he did have to attend the House of Commons to explain why he had ordered the sinking of the French vessels. After delivering his speech, Churchill was given a standing ovation from all sides of the House, even though just a few weeks earlier the War Cabinet had refused Churchill permission to carry out such an attack. This was a good example of just how quickly attitudes change in a time of war, and how one minute something is wrong, yet the same set of circumstances just a few weeks later are totally acceptable.

There were two questions that need asking here. Did Churchill have to attack the French fleet when he did, especially after having been given assurances by Admiral Marcel Gensoul that the French Fleet would never fall into the hands of the Germans? And what caused the War Cabinet to change its mind so dramatically about allowing Churchill to carry out his plan?

The reason for the sinking of the French fleet was possibly more involved than was first thought. After the escape of Belgian, British and French soldiers from the beaches of Dunkirk, there was a real fear of an imminent invasion by Nazi Germany, and it became apparent to Churchill that he needed warships to help fend off any such attack. The only nation he could sensibly turn to who could possibly provide him with a large number of such ships was America, who at the time were not in the war. Maybe because she hadn't decided if she was ever going to enter the war, or if so when and on whose side, she refused Churchill's request. This could have been because she wished to remain neutral. It could have been that after seeing what happened to the British at Dunkirk, America didn't think that it was good business to sell or loan warships to Britain, as they would likely be lost when Germany invaded.

Putting America's refusal to supply Churchill with warships to one side for the time being, I want to look at the attack on the French fleet for a moment. Maybe the attack took place for two reasons. Firstly, to send a strong message out to Germany that she was still a force to be reckoned with and could make such a strike, of her choosing, at any time or at any place she wanted, or maybe it was Churchill's way of sending a message to the Americans that Britain was still a force to be reckoned with, and she hadn't quite lost the war just yet. Maybe it was neither of these reasons, maybe it was because Churchill wanted the French warships for himself, to be handed over to the Royal Navy for immediate use, once new British crews had familiarised themselves with them.

Chapter 10

Coventry Blitz 1940

During the Second World War, Coventry was bombed by the German Luftwaffe on numerous occasions. Between August and October 1940, during the Battle of Britain, it was attacked a total of seventeen times. These attacks, which saw nearly 200 tons of bombs dropped on the city, killed 176 people, mainly civilians, and injured a further 680. There was a further Luftwaffe raid on the city on 17 October, but the most devastating one of all took place over the night of 14/15 November 1940. It was what the Germans codenamed Operation Moonlight Sonata, or *Mondscheinsonate* in German. In an attempt to destroy the city's factories and industrial infrastructure, 515 German bombers attacked Coventry.

After the initial wave of German aircraft successfully managed to drop marker flares on the locations that were to be bombed, the second, and much bigger wave of German aircraft attacked, dropping high explosive bombs across the city. These bombs caused massive craters in the roads making it difficult for the city's fire brigade and ambulances to get quickly to where they were needed to be, meaning that the death and destruction that the bombs created had even more impact.. The bombs also knocked out the city's water supply, electricity, gas and telephone lines.

High explosive bombs would always be dropped first to damage and blow up buildings, and once that had been achieved, the fires that were subsequently started by the incendiary bombs would take hold a lot quicker.

Germany could easily argue that Coventry was a legitimate military target, as it was one of the Midlands large industrial cities, where cars, bicycles, engines for aircraft and military munitions were all made. It also had a civilian population of over 235,000 people.

The question here of course is what did the Luftwaffe raids on Coventry have to do with Winston Churchill? This where an allegation of duplicity was made against him in relation to those very raids. Let me explain.

In June 1941, British Military Intelligence began using what became known as *Ultra,* to gain its wartime signals intelligence, which it obtained by intercepting and breaking high-level encrypted German and Japanese radio and teleprinter communications. The location where all this work was carried out was at the government's Code and Cypher School situated at Bletchley Park in Buckinghamshire.

The name *Ultra* didn't come from some fancy acronym, but rather its level of secrecy. The highest level of British security classification at the time was '*Most Secret*', but the quality of intelligence gained from the work undertaken by those who worked at Bletchley Park was deemed to be far more important than '*Most Secret*', so it was given the security clearance of '*Ultra Secret*' shortened to the word '*Ultra*'. So important was the work of Ultra that it remained secret until 1974.

During the Second World War, Frederick William Winterbotham held the rank of group captain in the RAF, with whom he had served since 1929 when he was assigned to the newly created Air Section of the Secret Intelligence Service, MI6.

He had served in the First World War, initially with the Royal Gloucestershire Regiment, but in 1916 he transferred to the Royal Flying Corps and became a fighter pilot. Whilst flying over Passchendaele on 13 July 1917 he was shot down and captured, and spent the rest of the war incarcerated as a prisoner of war. Most of his time was spent at Holzminden. His was a particularly interesting story, especially his military career from 1932, but his connection with this story is his wartime work as part of the *Ultra* team at Bletchley Park, and his book about his wartime work, *The Ultra Secret,* published in 1974. The book was the first one of its kind, talking in depth about the wartime secrets of Bletchley Park, *Ultra* and the Enigma machine. It explained his part in the programme, and provided a detailed and extensive account of how the large amount of Enigma-derived information was utilised to the Allies advantage across different theatres of war, including the Battle of the Atlantic.

Despite being at the very heart of British military intelligence, his book has been heavily criticised for a number of inaccuracies and the fact that he attempts to make his role in *Ultra* bigger and more important than it actually was. He acknowledges in the book that he was not a cryptologist and only had a basic knowledge of the cryptologic aspect of the *Ultra* operation.

It is because of his book that there is a connection with Winston Churchill, and the Luftwaffe attack on the city of Coventry on the night of 14/15 November 1940. Winterbotham claimed that Churchill and his government knew of the impending air attacks on Coventry, due to intelligence gained from German radio messages that had been encrypted with the Enigma machine and then decoded by staff at Bletchley Park. But despite this, Churchill ordered that no defensive measures should be put in place to try and defend Coventry, just in case the Germans suspected that their cipher had been broken.

As if Winterbotham wasn't a creditworthy individual in his own right, his version of accounts were supported by Sir William Stephenson, who was the Commander in Chief of all Allied intelligence during the Second World War, and had the code name of Intrepid. Stephenson worked closely with both Churchill and President Roosevelt, and met with both men on a regular basis. He claimed that both men knew in advance that Coventry was going to be bombed by the German Luftwaffe, but decided that they could not forewarn the British city, due to fear of the consequences if they did. Stephenson also claimed Churchill told him that the decision to let Coventry burn had aged him 'twenty years'.

There are others who were more closely involved in *Ultra* who hotly dispute what Winterbotham said in his book and the support that was afforded him by Stephenson. Peter John Ambrose Calvocoressi served as an intelligence officer, as well as being head of Air Section at Bletchley Park during the Second World War. His department was in charge of translating and analysing all deciphered Luftwaffe messages. Calvocoressi stated that *Ultra* never mentioned that Coventry was a target that was going to be attacked, and that Churchill did not know of the impending attack on Coventry. He had been informed that there was going to be an attack somewhere – just not the specific location. Even when he contemplated where it would take place, he believed the city most likely to be attacked was London.

However, since 1996 *Ultra* deciphers for the relevant period have been available at the UK's National Archives and one record shows that a German message was recorded and deciphered over 10 and 11 November 1940, which set out code words to be used by German aircraft on an operation named 'Mondschein Sonate,' which in English means Moonlight Sonata, a reference to a musical piece by the German composer Beethoven. The message contained neither a date for the air raid or the name of the city it was going to be on, and it certainly did not mention Coventry as the intended target. What it did say was that the transmission of the number '9' would denote the word, KORN, the code word for the city of Coventry, but this was not known at the time.

Churchill did not receive any new *Ultra* messages on the day of the Luftwaffe air raid on Coventry on 13/14 November 1940, because none had been intercepted. This being the case, the mystery surrounding why Winterbotham and Stephenson claimed Churchill did know about the impending German air raids on Coventry still remains.

Chapter 11

Fall of Singapore 1942

The surrender of Singapore during the Second World War has gone down as one of the worst defeats in British military history, and to an extent it was. If looked at on paper, the greater numerical advantage of the British and Allied forces should have had no problem dealing with a much smaller attacking Japanese force, but they did. This left two questions, how did it happen, and who was ultimately responsible for it?

Unbeknown to the British authorities, Japan had been planning the invasion of Singapore since July 1940, but they received some help in the shape of the German auxiliary cruiser *Atlantis*, which the Kriegsmarine knew as Schiff 16, a converted merchant vessel. On 11 November 1940, she captured the British steamer *Automedon* in the Indian Ocean. During a search of the *Automedon*, papers and documents intended for Air Marshal Sir Robert Brooke-Popham, who was the British Commander in the Far East, were found on her, which remarkably included detailed information about the weaknesses of the British naval base in Singapore. The following month, German authorities handed over those captured documents to the Japanese, which helped them to break British army codes, without the knowledge of British military authorities. But it didn't end there. In January 1941, the intelligence gathering wing of the Japanese Imperial Army managed to intercept and read a message that had been sent by British military authorities in Singapore to the War Ministry in London, which highlighted in great detail Singapore's weaknesses. The message about the island was so detailed and comprehensive, the Japanese did not believe it at first, instead thinking it was part of a British plan to trick them. It was only when they checked the content of the message against the documents that had been recovered from the *Automedon*, that they accepted its authenticity.

Japan's intentions were both ambitious and widespread, but her ongoing war with China since 1937, added to her everyday domestic consumption, had almost depleted her oil reserves. This left her with two options: firstly she could engage in diplomatic efforts to secure the quantities of oil that she required, or, if her diplomatic efforts failed, use military means to secure the same.

Having considered what to do, Japan decided to go ahead with the military option, which it has to be said was over-ambitious and implemented to the point of stupidity. Her plan to secure her required oil needs involved systematically attacking American, British and Dutch territories. This was such an ill thought out strategy by Japan, as at the time she was not at war with any of those three countries, but she must have worked out what the likely outcome would be in carrying out such attacks. After elements of the Imperial Japanese Navy attacked the large American naval base at Pearl Harbor in Hawaii on 7 December 1941, America declared war on Japan the very same day. After her forces then carried out attacks on Malaya, Singapore and Hong Kong, Britain responded in the same way, declaring war on Japan the following day. In the space of two days Japan now found herself at war with two of the world's super powers.

At the time of the attacks on the British controlled territories, Anthony Eden, who was the foreign secretary at the time, was on his way to Russia, so the Foreign Office was left in the hands of the prime minister. Churchill wrote the following letter which was sent to the Japanese Ambassador in London.

Sir,

On the evening of December 7th His Majesty's Government in the United Kingdom learned that Japanese forces without previous warning either in the form of a declaration of war or of an ultimatum with a conditional declaration of war, had attempted a landing on the coast of Malaya and bombed Singapore and Hong Kong.

In view of these wanton acts of unprovoked aggression committed in flagrant violation of International Law and particularly of Article 1 of the Third Hague Convention relative to the opening of hostilities, to which both Japan and the United Kingdom are parties, His Majesty's Ambassador in Tokyo has been instructed to inform the Imperial Japanese government in the name of his Majesty's Government in the United Kingdom, that a state of war exists between our two countries.

I have the honour to be, with high consideration.

Sir

Your obedient servant

Winston S Churchill.

When later challenged on the style of his writing in the letter, he replied, saying: 'Some people did not like this ceremonial style. But after all when you have to kill a man it costs nothing to be polite.'

What is interesting about this letter is more about what it doesn't say as opposed to what it does say. Nowhere in it is there an ultimatum with a conditional declaration of war if the ultimatum is not adhered to. It's a straightforward, 'our two countries are now at war' letter. There is no allowance of the possibility that it might have been rogue elements of the Japanese Imperial army and navy acting on their own, it was almost as if Churchill was happy to go to war with Japan as naively, he did not see them as a real threat, more a much weaker enemy who he could swat aside, quickly and easily, and then claim a great victory.

At this point I will deal with the why, as in why did Japan suddenly carry out the attacks on 7 December 1941? As previously mentioned, Japan and China had been at war since 1937, but China had the support of both Britain and America. In Japan's declaration of war against both the USA and Britain, she eloquently gave her reasons. The text of the declaration covers more than 600 words, but in essence says that she has been forced to resort to military action because the United States and the British Empire had engaged in 'disruptive actions against the Empire of Japan's foreign policy.' Furthermore, it said that the Japanese government had exhausted all avenues for averting war, despite the US imposing both oil and steel embargoes on her, which she took to be a hostile and provocative acts. It also mentioned that its ultimate goal was

75

the stability of East Asia and to contribute to world peace. It wanted to cultivate friendship among all nations and to enjoy prosperity in common with all nations.

Japan had only gone to war with China because of her disruptive behaviour throughout East Asia, only to then have the United States and Britain add their support behind China. The declaration did not however make any comment on the war crimes that her forces had committed in Nanking between 13 December 1937 and the end of January 1939, when a large number of Chinese civilians were massacred in the Chinese city. Estimates of those murdered range from 40,000 to 300,000. Whatever figure is correct there can be no excuse or acceptable reason for the Japanese forces to have carried out such systematic atrocities against Chinese civilians. Putting this aspect of her actions to one side for a moment, what if the United States and Britain had purposely placed restrictions upon Japan to strengthen their own positions throughout the region of South East Asia and the Pacific?

So let's compare Churchill's immediate declaration of war against Japan in 1941 with Chamberlain's ultimatum to Hitler in 1939. Nazi Germany had begun aggressively acquiring surrounding territories as early as 1936, beginning with the Rhineland area of Germany which had become a demilitarised zone under the conditions of the Treaty of Versailles which had ended the First World War. From there, Hitler decided to push matters further and invaded neighbouring Austria, the Sudetenland area of Czechoslovakia in 1938, before occupying the rest of Czechoslovakia in March 1939.

It would be fair to say that Hitler, by his actions, had pushed his luck, but on each occasion he had received a tepid reaction, so he continued. It was only in March 1939 after realising that Hitler was going to continue his invasions that Neville Chamberlain guaranteed Polish independence. On 1 September 1939, German troops and tanks crossed the Polish border. There then followed a period of mobilization of British and French troops, an action that was hoped would make Germany withdraw her troops, but it didn't. Mussolini even tried to intervene and prevent Hitler pushing matters to all-out war. There were even meetings between British and French diplomats and German Foreign Minister von Ribbentrop, who was warned that they would fulfil their obligation to Poland and go to war with Germany if it did not withdraw its forces from Poland.

At 9am on the morning of 3 September 1939, Britain's ambassador to Germany, Sir Neville Henderson, delivered an ultimatum to von Ribbentrop at the German Foreign Office in Berlin.

> More than twenty-four hours have elapsed since an immediate reply was requested to the warning of September 1st, and since then the attacks on Poland have been intensified. If his Majesty's Government has not received satisfactory assurances of the cessation of all aggressive action against Poland, and the withdrawal of German troops from that country, by 11 o'clock British Summer Time, from that time a state of war will exist between Great Britain and Germany.

German forces did not withdraw from Poland and the Second World War began in earnest. But it is an interesting comparison between the British response to Germany's actions and her response to the Japanese actions, just two years later.

Two things struck me about the comparison. Britain under the leadership of Chamberlain had some idea of the strength and capabilities of the enemy she was up against, and so trod carefully in her response. I will not go as far as to say Chamberlain feared or respected Hitler and Nazi Germany, but he was careful enough not to go blundering in with both feet. Secondly and maybe the more relevant of the two points, no part of Europe was a part of the British Empire, which meant she did not have the same major financial interests in the region – such as oil, rubber, tea, coffee, or mineral deposits – as she did in the Far East.

By the time Japan posed a threat in 1941, and with Churchill as the British prime minister, it was a totally different scenario. Partly because of financial interests in the region, but also because Churchill and the American President, Franklin Delano Roosevelt, did not believe that they were up against a formidable enemy in the form of the Japanese army and navy. How wrong they were.

Was it a case in 1941 of Britain and the US trying to treat Japan the same way that Nazi Germany had treated Britain and France in 1939?

Back to the Japanese planned attacks on American, British, and Dutch controlled territories in the Far East, Pacific, and Dutch East Indies. In the Far East, Malaya had much-needed rubber reserves, and via the Johore Straits, it was connected to the military strategic location of Singapore. In the Pacific there were the American territories of Guam, Wake Island, Gilbert Islands, and the Philippines, and in the Dutch East Indies were the oil-rich territories of Java and Borneo. Once these territories had been taken, Japan had planned for a period of consolidation to allow her to secure and build up the defences of the territories she had secured.

There was some interesting debate concerning Japan's actions in the Far East, in the Houses of Parliament on 8 December 1941. Part of what Churchill said was as follows:

> I do not yet know what part Siam or Thailand will be called upon to play in this fresh war, but a report has reached us that the Japanese have landed troops at Singora, which is in Siamese territory, on the frontier of Malaya, not far from the landing they had made on the British side of the frontier. Meanwhile, just before Japan had gone to war, I had sent the Siamese Prime Minister the following message. It was sent off on Sunday, early in the morning.

The message he referred to was worded as follows.

> There is a possibility of imminent Japanese invasion of your country. If you are attacked, defend yourself. The preservation of the full independence and sovereignty of Thailand is a British interest, and we shall regard you as if it were an attack on us.

These were strong words, but did they have any real substance to them. I do not have the figures for how many men there were in the Siamese Army in December 1941, but I am guessing there were no match for the invading Japanese forces. Churchill's words were certainly not backed up with any immediate offer or promise of British or Allied support.

Just eighteen days before Lieutenant Colonel Arthur Percival, General Officer Commanding Malaya Command – the man in charge of all British and Commonwealth troops in Malaya and Singapore – surrendered Singapore to the Japanese, Winston Churchill had deemed it necessary to ask the House of Commons for a vote of confidence for him and his government. The piece I am going to include from this motion is quite lengthy, but I feel that it provides value to the book to include it. The wording of the motion was such:

> That this House has confidence in His Majesty's Government and will aid it to the utmost in the vigorous prosecution of the War.

Just prior to his request for a vote of confidence, Churchill had been in the US on official business with President Roosevelt. The first member of the House to speak in the debate was Sir John Wardlaw-Milne, the MP for Kidderminster. Part of what he had to say, I found particularly interesting and relevant.

> The Prime Minister, strangely enough, put his request for a Vote of Confidence not primarily upon the necessity of a united front in the war, which is the one reason for it, to my mind, but partly on the ground that he must, above all things, be loyal to his colleagues. There are all kinds of loyalties in this world, and loyalty to colleagues is a splendid thing, but loyalty to the people and to the nation is greater still. I feel that the Prime Minister was unfortunate in the way in which he placed this request before us. It is not a case of asking him to jettison some of his team and to be disloyal to his colleagues. The Prime Minister has never had any difficulty before....

> The Prime Minister was not fair yesterday when he spoke about the chicken-heartedness on the part of those who would not vote against him. I repeat that there are bigger things than the composition of this government at stake, and one of them is the unity of all Allied peoples in the prosecution of the war.

Sir John's next words started getting more to the point in hand.

When the Prime Minister returned he could not have been surprised that he was met with considerable anxiety and unrest in the country, owing to the situation, particularly in the Far East. The country has been definitely misled. There is a feeling almost of horror that we should have been found unprepared, and apparently had learned so little from the last two years of war.

Statements have been made regarding our readiness to repel invasion at Singapore which were completely inaccurate. The Prime Minister was entirely correct when he said that he is the man responsible. I agree. I accept that statement, and I go further. I say that any criticism of any member of the government, as the government is at present constituted, becomes, unfortunately a criticism of the Prime Minister. If you live under a dictatorship, that must happen. We have two dictators, one a deputy-dictator dealing with the whole munitions programme here and abroad. Two hearts that beat as one.

We are told that the Prime Minister is entirely responsible and presumably, therefore, no blame must be attached to the people abroad. Does that mean that those who were in charge of our military, naval and other dispositions in the neighbourhood of Singapore were well aware of the inadequacy of our preparations and were making continued representations to the government regarding the position in which we were likely to be placed if Japan attacked? If it was so, surely there was no necessity for the flights of fancy in which these gentlemen in the Far East engaged. If fifty were making representations against the position at Singapore, and I am entitled to take that to be the position, they are in no way to blame. We must assume that they were making urgent representations regarding the state of affairs. Why then indulge in those flights of fancy? Let me give one illustration. There are many. An order of the day, quoted in the *Times* of 9th December, was issued by the Commander-in-Chief, Far East. It stated.

We are ready. We have had plenty of warning; our preparations have been made and tested. We are confident. Our defences are strong. Our weapons are efficient.

The MP for Lanark Northern, Captain Anstruther-Gray, interrupted with the following observation:

Surely my hon. Friend could not expect a Commander-in-Chief at that time to say we were unready.

Sir John replied:

I do not suggest that. I suggest that if the Commander-in-Chief knew that we were not ready, he should have kept his mouth shut. He is not a Minister of the Crown and is not bound to answer questions. It is not for members of the Fighting Services to make statements of that kind. There is no possible excuse, to my mind, for the statements that were made in the Far East. They have misled this country for months past. I am willing to say that the blame rests upon the government, and I have said so.

Sir John went on to explain how he understood that senior officers in Singapore had been put in a really difficult position by politicians, but they knew the real situation in Singapore, and for whatever reason had decided to perpetuate the lie that everything was alright, when they knew full well that it most certainly was not. He felt that they would have been better off simply saying nothing at all.

It was Churchill's decision to ultimately support Russia and Libya with tanks and aircraft at the expense of the defence of Singapore. This left Singapore without a single tank, and a greatly reduced number of aircraft, which she undoubtedly needed for her own defence. It was sad to think that Churchill thought it more important to keep Stalin and

Russia happy than he did to defend Singapore. What was even more unforgiveable was that Churchill knew full well that Japan was still at war with China, and that there were a large number of Chinese amongst the population of Singapore. By the time the Japanese had surrendered Singapore in 1945, it is estimated that upwards of 50,000 Chinese men on Singapore had been murdered or were missing. Churchill had viewed the European war as being much more important than anything that was taking place in the Far East, no matter what the cost in human life.

Churchill had informed the House the previous day that there were some 60,000 troops on Singapore after some two years of war. What Sir John wanted to know from Churchill was why had there not been more troops sent to Singapore, and why had some of those who were there not been sent to Malaya to bolster their defences.

Sir John then turned to comments that had been made, drawing a comparison between Pearl Harbor and Singapore. He pointed out that the Americans had been caught napping at Pearl Harbor, but at least they could use the excuse that they were not at war with Japan at the time of the attack. Britain was at war with Japan and was still caught napping. He highlighted the fact that MPs had never had an explanation about what happened to the *Repulse* and the *Prince of Wales,* and why they had been sent out to sea without any air protection at all.

He also highlighted how members of the House, along with the prime minister had known of the potential threat posed by Japan for at least two years. That being the case, why wasn't more done to secure Singapore and make it an impregnable fortress? Members had spent the last two years encouraging the prime minister and the government to at least provide aid to China to allow her to defend herself against the Japanese, because the stronger Chinese forces were, the more of a problem they would pose for the Japanese, which would help curtail Japan's military activities throughout the Far East and the Pacific.

Sir John wanted to know from the prime minister the consideration (if any) he and his government had given to the possibility of Japanese forces occupying Indo-China. He also wanted to know what if anything had been done defensively when Japanese forces began landing in Thailand. Soon after their forces had landed, they had begun building aerodromes, adding to the ones they had built in Indo-China, as well as along the borders with Malaya. Once this was known, Sir Henry asked if any attempt had been made to prepare a defence against an attack from that direction or send troops to prepare for an attack.

He was now in full swing and wasn't holding back as Churchill and his ministers must have been squirming in their seats.

> The real defence of Singapore is not only against the sea but also against the land. Singapore bears the same relationship to the mainland of Malaya, to Johore as the Isle of Wight does to the coast of Hampshire.

One of the problems with the defence of Singapore is that it was only properly defended from attack from the sea. Because of the dense jungles of Malaya in particular, it wasn't believed that an invasion of Singapore would be land-based via Malaya, it just wasn't taken as a serious possibility.

On the night of 7/8 December 1941, three Japanese transport ships, the *Awazisan Maru, Ayatosan Maru,* and the *Sakura Maru,* which collectively had some 5,200 troops of the Takumi Detachment under the command of Major General Hiroshi Takumi, most of whom were veteran soldiers of the war with China, were seen by patrolling Indian soldiers of the 8th Indian Infantry Brigade, at anchor about 2 miles from the beaches at Kota Bharu.

To make the beaches a hostile location to try and land, the Indian defences included artillery pieces, machine guns, minefields and barbed wire. Although the first two waves of Japanese soldiers ashore sustained heavy casualties, eventually they sustained, breached the Indian defences and landed. By 9 May, the Japanese had captured Kota Bharu town, despite a spirited defence by the Indian defenders.

Back in Parliament, Sir John continued his attack, bombarding Winston Churchill with question after question in relation to Singapore.

> Again, is it true, I ask the government, that the invasion of Kota Bharu was foretold to the military authorities in Singapore months ago and that they were warned then that this was exactly what would happen? Did they take any precautions? I have here a long letter from which I am permitted to quote, a distinguished officer who was defence

Security Officer in Malaya. I prefer not to give his name as he is, as I say, a distinguished officer and is now serving in another capacity. I trust I may read some passages from the letter, which is dated 14 December 1941.

It can be no great secret that the defences of Singapore consisted entirely of precautions against attack from the sea. A single battalion used to garrison the naval base which is the sole importance of Singapore. The base lies between Singapore and the mainland of Malaya; the not even federated State of Johore. Northward from the open roadstead of the base there were no defences, no troops, scarcely police either. A long coast-line, unprotected, unpatrolled except by occasional aircraft. Great stretches of beach as much as two miles in breadth and hard as cement offered landing grounds for surprise from the air and seizure of a bridgehead. With three weeks' command of the sea, the Japanese could land at Kota Bharu, at Kwantan and at Mersing. No troops, no precautions anywhere.

Sir John accused the prime minister and his government of 'having misled the country' in relation to Singapore. He finished by saying:

To my mind that is the reason for the vote of confidence and the only reason why it should be given, but it does not alter the fact that the House is entitled to get from the government a far more detailed explanation of what has happened in the Far East than it has to date.

Clearly there were many who were not happy with Winston Churchill and his government as to what they had or hadn't done in relation to Singapore, but why he left it so poorly defended has never been fully or properly answered.

The Battle of Singapore started on 8 December 1942, after Japanese forces had crossed the Johore Straits. A staggering figure to note is by that time, there were only ten serviceable Allied aircraft left to help in the defence of Singapore. They were Hawker Hurricane fighter aircraft of No. 232 Squadron based at RAF Kallang. By the end of the following day there were no Allied aircraft flying in the skies over Singapore.

Why Churchill didn't see fit to provide the defenders of Singapore with sufficient aircraft, or why there were no tanks on the island has never been fully explained. This is particularly poignant as at the same time Churchill was happily sending a large number of tanks to Russia to help Stalin in their fight against Germany. Remember this is the same Russia who had signed the German-Soviet Non-aggression Pact on 23 August 1939, in which the countries agreed not to take military action against each other for the next ten years. That pact was subsequently broken by Germany, when as part of Operation Barbarossa, she invaded Russia on 22 June 1941.

In my opinion, Churchill let Singapore and its people down extremely badly. This was a Crown Colony, from which Churchill and his government would have expected and demanded loyalty, but Churchill was not prepared or willing to provide the same level of commitment in return. To support my opinion I offer a missive that Churchill sent to Field Marshal Archibald Wavell on the evening of 10 February 1942.

I think you ought to realise the way we view the situation in Singapore. It was reported to cabinet by the Chief of the Imperial General Staff, General Alan Brooke, that Percival has over 100,000 men, of whom 33,000 are British and 17,000 Australian. It is doubtful whether the Japanese have as many in the whole Malay Peninsula. In these circumstances the defenders must greatly out number Japanese forces who have crossed the straits, and in a well-contested battle they should destroy them. There must at this stage be no thought of saving the troops or sparing the population. The battle must be fought to the bitter end at all costs. The 18th Division has a chance to make its name in history. Commanders and senior officers should die with their troops. The honour of the British Empire and of the British Army is at stake. I rely on you to show no mercy to weakness in any form. With the Russians fighting as they are and the Americans so stubborn at Luzon, the whole reputation of our country and our race is involved. It is expected that every unit will be brought into close contact with the enemy and fight it out.

Churchill's message to Wavell was a disgrace and an insult to the population of Singapore, as well as the British and Allied soldiers who were ultimately wounded, killed and captured, having been sent there to defend it. After having failed to adequately train and equip the military personnel who had been sent to protect the Crown Colony, he expected them to fight to the death.

Later that same night, Wavell was about to board a flying boat from Singapore on route to Java, when he slipped as he stepped out of his staff car, fell and broke two bones in his back.

Churchill spoke of fighting to the last man so as to save the honour of the British army and the British Empire, when what he really meant to say was that he expected the military personnel on Singapore to fight to the death, in an effort to save his own reputation.

Besides the 80,000 estimated Allied soldiers who were captured and taken prisoners of war at Singapore, a further 5,000 were either killed or wounded.

Amongst the senior officers there was much blame apportioned to different individuals amidst their group. As well as Percival for being the man who made the final decision to surrender, some were accused of dithering, some of cracking under the pressure, and some of making poor military decisions.

It strikes me that there was a lack of leaders who were prepared to stand and fight. Many of the Allied senior officers did not have a natural fighting spirit or a real desire to engage the enemy. But the Battle of Singapore hadn't just been lost in the days between 8 and 15 February 1942. It had been lost long before then because of British arrogance in underestimating the Japanese, along with an inability to properly build sufficient defensive positions on all sides of the Island. There was then a lack of properly trained and equipped military personnel to defend it. There may well have been in the region of 100,000 British and Allied troops on the island, but a large number of British, Australia, and Indian troops had not received sufficient military training to deal with what they had been sent there to do, as well as never having previously been in battle.

In closing this chapter I will also point out that in 1936, Major General William Dobbie, who was then the General Officer Commanding Malaya, wanted to know if mainland Malaya required more military personnel to defend it. He gave the task of coming up with a tactical assessment of how the Japanese might attack, to his Chief Staff Officer, who at the time was Colonel Archibald Percival. In 1937, Percival determined that the most likely location for the Japanese to land was north Malaya. They would then probably come ashore on beaches in both Thailand and Malaya, capture nearby aerodromes so that they could speedily gain air superiority. This would then lead to further Japanese troops being landed in the area of Johore to enable them to intercept northbound communications and build another base in the North Borneo area, and from there Japan could make amphibious landings in east Singapore in the Changi area of the island. Percival's appraisal was forwarded via Dobbie to the War Office, along with an additional report from Dobbie for the construction of fixed defensive positions in southern Johore. No such defensive positions were ever acted upon, and the region remained as it was before Percival had carried out his appraisal in 1937.

In 1941, Percival was promoted to the rank of acting Lieutenant General and appointed as the General Officer Commanding Malaya, having replaced his previous boss, Dobbie. Despite now being in charge, none of his previous recommendations had been acted upon, and he does not appear to have done anything to rectify that position.

Percival had not exactly been overjoyed at his new appointment. He was in a somewhat Catch 22 situation. On the one hand he was concerned that if there was no war in the Far East, he could hold that position for many years in what would be left as a far-off post of the British Empire. But if there was a war, his concerns were that he would be embroiled in a fight with insufficient numbers of manpower to be adequately able to defend themselves, as was the way with such posts in distant locations of the empire, especially at the beginning of a conflict. He wasn't wrong in his belief, but the question is why didn't he challenge Churchill and his government on those very points, and if he did why didn't he push the point time and again until he received sufficient forces and equipment?

Whether Churchill was correct in sending men, tanks and aircraft, which were also needed in Singapore, to Russia and the Middle East, is a separate debate, but by doing so he also helped greatly in the demise of Singapore.

On 19 February 1942, Petty Officer A.P. Herbert, MP, asked the prime minister in the House of Commons, if he would appoint a court of inquiry to look into the retreats of the British army from Dunkirk, Norway, Greece, Crete, Malaya and Benghazi, presided over by a High Court Judge. Clement Atlee, who at the time was the deputy prime minister in the wartime coalition government, simply replied 'No, sir.'

On Wednesday, 16 April 1942, Winston Churchill gave a speech at the House of Commons concerning the fall of Singapore and the situation of the war in the Far East. The House went into Secret Session to hear what he had to say and by the time he had finished he had left all of those in attendance, in a sombre mood.

It was one of the longest and most detailed wartime speeches that Churchill ever made. He held nothing back. Every last detail of the debacle was laid bare as he revealed all. He began about talking about the loss of HM ships *Ark Royal, Barham, Prince of Wales, Repulse* and how the Royal Navy battleships were damaged and put out of action. This meant that in just seven weeks, a third of all Britain's battleships and light cruisers had been either lost or put out of action.

He went on to reveal that 100,000 British and Allied troops had been captured and taken prisoners of war when they surrendered to a force of just 30,000 Japanese. His next point was interesting. It was one of those 'take the bull by the horns' moments. Rather than wait to be asked, which he knew he would be, he explained that despite being shocked at the surrender, he had decided against the idea of instigating an enquiry into the disaster as it would hamper the prosecution of the war still being fought in other areas of the world. The real reason for not carrying out such an enquiry was more likely because it would reveal the part he and his government played in being largely responsible for the debacle that had led to the island's defenders being in such a position where they even felt the need to surrender.

I do not intend to include the content of his entire speech on these pages, as not all of it was directly about Singapore and not all of it was relevant to the aspect of Churchill I am writing about.

The start of his speech was a brief overview of the problems faced in the region.

> Since Japan became our enemy and the United States our
> Ally, after December 7, the weight of the war upon us has
> become far more severe and we have sustained a painful

series of misfortunes in the Far East. Apart from the stubborn and brave defence of the Bataan Peninsula by the United States, the brunt of the Japanese attacks has fallen almost entirely upon us and the Dutch.

The United States fleet has not yet regained the command of the Pacific which was lost after Pearl Harbor; and while we are at war with Germany and Italy we do not possess the naval resources necessary to maintain the command of the Indian Ocean against any heavy detachment from the main Japanese fleet.

Before the Japanese entered the war, we were already fully extended in the North Sea, Atlantic and Mediterranean theatres by sea, land and air. We have drawn all possible forces to meet our new, fresh, and most formidable antagonist. But in spite of all we could do and the risks we ran and are running, we have been and are at present outnumbered by the sea, land and air forces of Japan throughout the Far Eastern theatre. This fact must be faced by all who wish to understand what has happened and what is going to happen.

Churchill made no mention in his speech of the tanks that he had removed from Singapore or the additional aircraft that had been asked for by the island's senior military personnel and refused. Neither was there a breakdown of the numbers and nationalities of the military personnel who were present on the island and their battle readiness. Many of the soldiers who had been sent to the island had never seen any kind of military action, let alone had to face up to a fanatical and well-drilled enemy like the Japanese.

Reading this first part of his speech made me realise just how fortunate the British were that Japan decided to attack the Americans at Pearl Harbor. Without America in the war, the Japanese would have quickly overrun the Pacific and Far East regions, coming up against little or no opposition on the way. This also throws up the point: that without American assistance the war in Europe would have gone on for much longer, with no guarantee that Britain and her Allies would have even beaten the Germans. The knock-on effect of this was that a return to the Far East and the Pacific by Britain and her allies would have been delayed by maybe a couple of years, if not longer, by which time the Japanese would have had a much stronger foothold in the region and would have been much more difficult to dislodge.

The next part of his speech was a surprising admission of either his imperialistic arrogance or his inability to properly judge the full extent of an enemy.

> I frankly admit that the violence, fury, skill and might of Japan has far exceeded anything that we had been led to expect. The Japanese military performances in China had not seemed remarkable. The Chinese had always been a weak nation, divided, and traditionally unwarlike. We knew that they were ill-armed and ill-supplied, especially with every weapon that matters in modern war. And yet for four and a half years the Japanese, using as many as a million men at a time, had failed to quell or conquer them.

> Neither of course were we prepared for the temporary eclipse and paralysis of the United States sea power in the Pacific, which followed from the disaster at Pearl Harbor.

It was because of Churchill's misjudgement of Japan's full capability that led him to detour much needed men and equipment that were due for Singapore, and send them to other theatres of war in Russia and Libya, where the fight was against Germany. This wasn't the first time he had misjudged an enemy's true military capabilities, by that I am referring to the disaster of Gallipoli in 1915 and 1916, when British and Allied forces suffered the indignity and embarrassment of being defeated by Turkish forces, and then having to extricate themselves from the peninsula, under the cover of darkness, but sadly, once again, albeit this time with the Japanese as the enemy, he did not appear to have learnt his lesson.

The next part of his speech appears somewhat at odds with the actual reality of the situation, which then makes it quite a naïve and shocking statement to make. I will include the entire paragraph, all of which is relevant, but I will highlight some specific words to show where my shock is focused.

> In spite of the results up to date, **I remain convinced that the broad strategic dispositions which we made of our forces prior to the Japanese attack, and the redistributions made after that attack, were the best in our power**. Sometimes, though not always, people are wise after the event, but it is also possible to be wise before the event and yet not have the power to stop it happening. In war, misfortunes may come from faults or errors in the High Command. They may also come from the enemy being far too strong or fighting far too well.

I am not quite sure how Churchill can claim Singapore was as it should have been prior to the Japanese attack. It was not fit for purpose. It didn't have a sufficient number of experienced fighting men, tanks or aircraft with which to properly defend itself, and its main defensive guns were pointing out to sea, because an attack from Malaya had not been foreseen. If Churchill truly felt that was the best deployment and use of British and Allied military forces prior to the Japanese invasion of Singapore, then I am staggered.

Churchill then went on to talk about the loss of two of the Royal Navy's vessels who were involved at Singapore.

> HMS *Prince of Wales* and HMS *Repulse* arrived at Singapore on December 2, 1941, this seemed to be a timely moment. It was hoped that their presence there might be deterrent upon the war party in Japan, and it was intended that they should vanish as soon as possible into the blue. I have already explained to the House how they became involved in a local operation against Japanese transports in the Gulf of Siam which led to their destruction.

What Churchill had conveniently forgotten to add to this part of his statement was that he had publicly announced that the *Prince of Wales* and the *Repulse* were being sent to Singapore to deter the Japanese. The phrase 'red rag to a bull' immediately comes to mind. Japan's response came in the shape of Admiral Isoroku Yamamoto, who sent 36 Mitsubishi G4M bomber aircraft to reinforce his Air Group already in the area.

With the Japanese threatening to overrun Malaya, Admiral Sir Tom Philips was pressed to use the *Prince of Wales* and the *Repulse* in an offensive role, to try and intercept and destroy Japanese invasion convoys in the South China Sea, on their way to Malaya. On 10 December, having knowingly and willingly set sail without any kind of air cover, both ships were attacked by land-based bomber aircraft along with torpedo bombers of the Imperial Japanese Navy. The loss of these two Royal Navy vessels severely weakened the British Eastern Fleet in Singapore.

Yet again Churchill was somewhat economical with the truth. He failed to mention that the *Prince of Wales* and the *Repulse* had deployed to attack a main Japanese invasion force that was heading for the Malayan coastline. He had also omitted to inform the House that the two vessels had been in the open sea without any air cover at the time they were attacked by Japanese aircraft. In fairness to Churchill he had no control over Admiral Philips' decision to take to sea without any air cover, but that still doesn't explain why Churchill didn't tell the House about this, or the fact that as a result of the two ships being sunk, 840 officers and men had been killed.

About halfway through his speech, Churchill covered a point that many present would have no doubt been seeking to have put in place.

In all these circumstances I do not wonder that requests should be made for an inquiry by a Royal Commission, not only into what took place upon the spot in the agony of Singapore but into all the arrangements which had been made beforehand. I am convinced however, that this would not be good for the country, and that it would hamper the prosecution of the war. Australian accounts reflect upon the Indian troops. Other credible witnesses disparage the Australians. The lack of any effective counter attack by the 18th Division which arrived in such high spirits and good order, and never seem to have had their chance, is criticised. The Generalship is criticised. There is an endless field for recrimination. Most of those concerned are prisoners. General Wavell, who was in charge of the whole ABDA area from January 15 onwards, is far too busy grappling with new perils. We too have enough trouble on our hands to cope with the present and the future, and I could not in any circumstances consent to adding such a burden, for a heavy burden it would be, to those which we have to bear. I must ask the House to support the government in this decision, which is taken in any ignoble way to shield individuals or safeguard the administration but solely in the interests of the state and for the successful prosecution of the war. The premature fall of Singapore led to failures of the resistance in Java and Sumatra. But this might have happened in any case in view of the decisive Japanese superiority in numbers and organisation.

As I have said elsewhere in this book, I believe Churchill's words here were nothing more than an attempt to save his own political career. He had experienced at first hand, in the aftermath of the Gallipoli campaign of 1915/1916, when he was forced out of his political position, what could come out of such an enquiry. He makes the excuse that there was a war going on and it wasn't the right time, yet during the First World War there was still a war going on when the enquiry into the Gallipoli campaign was undertaken. Yet again, not one of Churchill's finest moments.

In 1944, Captain Leonard David Gammans, the Conservative MP for Hornsey in North London, wrote a 32-page booklet entitled, *Singapore Sequel*. Page 4 included the following sentence: 'It is a thousand pities that no British statesman has thought fit to explain these events, either in Parliament or on the radio.'

Other than Churchill's speech to the House of Commons in a Secret Session on 23 April 1942, to this day there has never been a public enquiry into why Singapore fell so easily. Even after the war it was never picked up on, and now, well, it has been too late for many years and there is no longer any point in taking that point any further. It has simply been left to historians to discuss and argue the rights and wrongs of what Churchill did in relation to Singapore.

Chapter 12

Bengal Famine of 1943

By and large, Winston Churchill is remembered in the eyes of the British public for the heroic stance he took against Nazi Germany, during those far-off days of the Second World War. He is held in such high esteem for ensuring that Great Britain, as a nation, didn't lose the war and fall under German control. It would be fair to say that if Winston Churchill hadn't been prime minister of the United Kingdom, Nazi Germany would have either won the war, or those in charge of the country would have either surrendered, or worked out some kind of deal with Hitler and his cronies to stay out of the war. But Churchill's stock wasn't always so high.

In 1943 during the Second World War, what history has recorded as the Bengal famine took place. Out of the nation's population of over 60 million people, some 3 million people who were living in the country's Bengal province, in what at the time was British India, died. What killed them wasn't bullets or bombs, but a combination of malaria, starvation and other similar diseases. At the time of the starvation, not only was Churchill the prime minister of the United Kingdom, but of British India as well.

The famine came about in the main because Churchill and his government ordered the diversion of much-needed food from already under-fed Indians, so that it could be stockpiled in Britain and Europe. At its peak during the Second World War, Britain had stockpiled 18.5 million tons of food and raw materials. So vast were some of the stockpiles of raw materials that they were too much even for the warehouses that had been allocated for their storage.

Churchill didn't appear to have too much in the way of common humility for the Indian people, and he didn't always hide his feelings on the topic either. During the height of the war, Churchill received an urgent telegram from the authorities in Delhi, informing him of the numbers of people who had died as a result of the famine. One might expect such a message to have been met with a sympathetic ear, shock maybe or even utter disbelief, Churchill's only response was to enquire as to why Gandhi hadn't yet died.

The main aim of imperialism is for a controlling nation to increase its own wealth and standards of living, by utilising the controlled nation's own natural resources. In Britain's case her control over India had long since been justified with the pretence, or lie, that her presence and control in the country was in place for the benefit of the Indian people. If one were able to accept and believe that premise was actually true, then how was the Bengal famine ever allowed to take place?

It is said that at a British War Cabinet meeting in 1943, during the time of the famine, Churchill had said, 'The famine was their own fault for breeding like rabbits.' He had once made comments to the Secretary of State for India and Burma, Leopold Amery, which left it abundantly clear that he was no great lover of the Indian people.

Amery was the Secretary of State for India and Burma between 13 May 1940 and 26 July 1945, which was the same period of time that Churchill was the British prime minister. Amery was a somewhat intriguing choice, as the two men had long disagreed over India, but maybe the choice was more to do with the fact that Amery had previously been the Secretary of State for the Colonies between 6 November 1924 and 4 June 1929.

Amery often found Churchill's attitude and views of India and its people, far removed from his own, and his memoirs went as far as to say, 'Churchill knew "as much of the Indian problem as George III did of the American colonies".'

What made the situation in India even more difficult to understand, is that at the same time she was in the throes of a famine, her own grain was also being exported to what was then Ceylon, and is now Sri Lanka. That just added even more confusion to the situation as there was no threat of famine in Ceylon at that time. As if to rub salt to the wounds, wheat that was plentiful in Australia was being shipped past India to large ports and depots in the Mediterranean and Balkans areas. If that wasn't bad enough the British government prevented India from importing much-needed food, either by purchasing it or using her own ships to bring the same into the country. The final straw in what had already become the inexplicable behaviour of the British government towards India, came about when the former willingly and knowingly purchased grain on the world's open markets, at greatly inflated prices. This made it almost impossible for ordinary Indian people to be able to afford to buy grain.

Why Winston Churchill and the British government had conducted themselves in this manner towards the Indian people, has never been admitted. In the circumstances I believe this gives people the right to draw their own conclusions, but in the cold light of day, it didn't look good back then and it still doesn't look good now.

In addition to Churchill's questionable approach on the matter, it has to be said that the extent of the famine and the death toll that followed, was made worse because of the Japanese capture of Burma, a country which for India had previously been a primary source for food imports, especially rice. Once the Japanese arrived, that had abruptly come to an end.

There wasn't just one reason for the Bengal famine of 1943, but undoubtedly the decisions taken by Churchill and his government did not help the situation at all. What makes it so scandalous is that Churchill must have been aware of the large number of unnecessary Indian deaths that had taken place as a result of the famine, mainly because of his decisions, yet despite this, he continued with the same approach, knowing that more would surely die. The question is, why?

What makes the Bengal famine even more grotesque is that it didn't come about because of a drought, which although sad, was an 'act of God', it happened mainly because of British government policy towards India and her people, and was totally avoidable.

The Viceroy and Governor General of India between 1 October 1943 and 21 February 1947, was Field Marshal Archibald Edmund Wavell, appointed to the position by Churchill and his government, but despite this he most certainly was not a 'yes' man, nor did he hold their views on India. He was at a loss to understand their take on why they were being unhelpful as they were. Wavell said of Churchill and his government, that they were 'negligent, hostile and contemptuous', in their attitude towards India. One of Wavell's first actions as Viceroy was to deal with the Bengal famine, by ordering the army to distribute much-needed foods to the starving Bengali people. The obvious question is why couldn't that have been done sooner?

It would be fair to say that Wavell felt an affinity with India, Indian culture and its people, having previously served as its Commander-in-Chief.

Wavell was replaced as Viceroy of India by Lord Mountbatten after the British Prime Minister, Clement Atlee, had 'lost confidence' in him. This was a strange decision leading up to Indian independence as of 15 August 1947, which also saw the birth, at the same time, of Pakistan. During his time as viceroy, Wavell had tried to move the debate on Indian independence forward as best he could, but he received little in the way of support from either Winston Churchill or his successor, Clement Atlee, with Churchill vehemently opposed to Indian independence.

Wavell died in London on 24 May 1950, and in keeping with his forty-two years of military service, which had seen him involved in the Second Boer War, the First World War, as well as the Second World War, he was awarded a funeral with full military honours. After his death, his body lay in state at the Tower of London prior to his funeral service at Westminster Abbey. To show the level of esteem in which he was held, Wavell's funeral possession travelled along the River Thames from the Tower of London to Westminster Pier. The last time that had happened was in 1806 at the funeral of Horatio Nelson.

Clement Atlee, Lord Halifax (who at the beginning of the Second World War had been the Secretary of State for Foreign Affairs), Field Marshal Bernard Montgomery, Field Marshal Alan Francis Brooke, and numerous other military and political figures were present but one very noticeable individual who wasn't in attendance was Winston Churchill even though he was once again prime minister. There might very well have been a very good reason why he did not attend the funeral, but equally, it could have simply been because he did not want to go.

Chapter 13

Dresden Bombings 1945

Between 13 and 15 February 1945, as the war in Europe entered its final few months, bomber aircraft from the Royal Air Force (RAF) and the United States Army Air Forces (USAAF) attacked the German city of Dresden, resulting in a devastating loss of civilian life, as well as a large number of casualties.

There were a total of four raids which involved 722 heavy bombers of the RAF, and 527 from the USAAF who between them dropped a total of 3,900 tons of high-explosive bombs and incendiary devices on the city. More than 1,600 acres of the city centre were destroyed in the bombing and the resulting firestorm.

The actual number of people killed in the bombings has always been a bone of contention, with figures varying from 22,700 to 500,000, depending on which source is believed. In March 1945, the Nazi authorities ordered their newspapers to publish an estimated death toll of up to 500,000 and casualties in the region of 200,000, but as recently as 2010, Dresden City Council commissioned a study into the numbers of those killed, and came up with an estimated figure of 25,000; roughly the same figure as city authorities at the time of the bombings. As there were an estimated 200,000 German refugees in and around the centre of Dresden at the time of the attacks, the exact death toll of the raids is unlikely ever to be known.

Besides the four main attacks of 13-15 February, the Americans carried out a further three attacks on the city, two of which took place on 2 March 1945, both of which targeted the city's railway marshalling yards. The third attack, aimed at industrial areas of the city, took place on 17 April. Critics of the bombing have claimed that the aerial attacks were nothing more than indiscriminate area bombing, that were not proportionate to any military gains that may or may not have been made.

It was further claimed that Dresden was nothing more than a cultural landmark, with little or no strategic importance.

It has also been claimed that the attacks were nothing more than targeted attacks on a civilian population with the sole intention of harming the morale of the German people. The knock-on effect of the attacks was that it reduced the amount of German housing and greatly added to the German refugee problems.

Regardless of what happened at Dresden, maybe the more pertinent question is why did it actually take place? The war was fast coming to an end, and Russian forces were just 70 kilometres from Berlin as of 8 February 1945, the time that they crossed the River Oder. At around the same time, a report was prepared for Winston Churchill by the British Joint Intelligence Sub-committee, entitled *German Strategy and Capacity to Resist.* The report, so secret it was marked for Churchill's eyes only, estimated that Germany would only be able to hold out until about the middle of April 1945 if Russian forces overran her eastern defences, but if the Germans managed to prevent the Russians from taking Silesia, they might be able to hold out for several more months. Churchill and his commanders determined that any help that could be provided to the Russians on the Eastern Front would undoubtedly shorten the war, and save thousands of Allied lives.

In August 1944, an Allied operation, Thunderclap, was drawn up with a view to carrying out a massive aerial bombardment of Berlin. The plan estimated that the raids would result in the deaths of 110,000 key German personnel, with a similar number of people being injured. Although a number of these would be military and Nazi party members, many would be civilians. The ultimate purpose of the raid was to affect German morale. After the plan was considered in more detail, it was shelved and never took place. The plan was revisited in early 1945, but once again it did not go ahead.

Air Commodore Sydney Button, who was the RAF's director of bomber operations, sent a memo to Sir Norman Bottomley, Deputy Chief of the Air Staff. The memo was dated 22 January 1945. The idea was for a coordinated air attack on nominated German cities by the RAF, which it was hoped would have a twofold effect. Firstly, it was hoped that it would have a massive negative effect on German morale, both militarily and civilian-wise, and secondly, that it would assist the Russian offensive on the Eastern Front. Three days after the memo was received by Sir Norman Bottomley, the Joint Intelligence Committee supported the plan as it tied in nicely with the military-based intelligence that the British held regarding large numbers of German infantry divisions being on the move from their deployments in the east to reinforce the Eastern Front in the fight against the Russians. It had become a matter of high priority to delay, disrupt or destroy the German forces and their supplies from reaching that destination.

The Air Officer Commanding Bomber Command, Arthur 'Bomber' Harris, who was an ardent supporter of area bombing, was asked for his opinion on the matter. His reply wasn't just 'yes,' but a resounding one. He put forward the proposal that simultaneous attacks were carried out on the German cities of Chemnitz, Leipzig and Dresden. The same evening that Harris came up with his suggestion, Winston Churchill contacted Sir Archibald Sinclair, Secretary of State for Air, and asked him what plans had been drawn up to carry out Harris's proposals. Sinclair expediently passed on Churchill's enquiry to Sir Charles Portal, who was the Chief of the Air Staff. Portal's answer was thus:

> We should use available effort in one big attack on Berlin and attacks on Dresden, Leipzig, and Chemnitz, or any cities where a severe blitz will not only cause confusion in the evacuation from the east, but will also hamper the movement of troops from the West.

Portal added that he believed that aircraft used for any such planned raid should not be diverted away from their current primary role of destroying oil-production facilities, enemy aircraft factories and submarine pens. Although Portal's answer was a very succinct one, Churchill was not impressed with it, and spoke again with Sir Archibald Sinclair, on 26 January 1945 requesting a plan of operations.

> I asked last night whether Berlin, and no doubt other large cities in East Germany, should not now be considered especially attractive targets. Pray report to me tomorrow (about) what is going to be done.

Churchill's stern response left Sinclair clear of mind in what he needed to do. He wasted no time in contacting Deputy Chief of the Air Staff, Sir Norman Bottomley, who in turn was similarly quick in contacting Arthur 'Bomber' Harris, and asked him to carry out attacks on Berlin, Dresden, Leipzig and Chemitz as soon as was possible, 'With the particular object of exploiting the confused conditions which are likely to exist in the above mentioned cities during the successful Russian advance.'

So it was that on 27 January 1945 Sinclair was able to inform Churchill that the air strikes he requested to be carried out on the previously mentioned German cities, in an effort to disrupt the civilian population during their evacuation from the east, and German troop movements from the west, would go ahead. It was just a case of when.

Churchill had certainly sped proceedings up somewhat by his desire to get raids on nominated German cities underway, as on 31 January, Sir Norman Bottomley sent a message to Sir Charles Portal, informing him that large bombing raids on Dresden and other German cities would be extremely useful as such attacks would hamper Germany's attempts to move reinforcements around so freely, and civilian evacuations would simply add to the confusion by clogging up the same routes needed for the free movement of soldiers and equipment. They had learnt that much from the Luftwaffe raids on Coventry throughout 1940. Such damage to a city's civilian infrastructure was believed to have more impact than an attack on a legitimate military target such as a factory.

The chaos and disruption caused when cities were bombed had a major effect on the civilian population at all levels. Besides the loss of all utilities, communications, food and water, there was little or nothing in the way of leadership, meaning people were not knowing where to go or when. They had two options: remain where they were amongst the rubble of what was once their home – but in doing so, they were left not knowing if the RAF or USAAF would return the following evening to finish off the job – or they could leave not knowing which direction to go, as they had no idea which town or city would be bombed next. Hence chaos ruled.

By January 1945, Dresden, which was Germany's seventh largest city had not previously been bombed by the Allies, which in itself is quite remarkable taking into account that it was one of the nation's foremost industrial areas. In 1944, according to the German Army High Command, there were 127 factories and other similar workshops connected to the German war effort situated in the Dresden area.

In December 1978, the American authorities released a classified wartime report in relation to the 1944 Dresden attacks, which had been written in response to concerns about the rights and wrongs of the raid. In their report, the Americans wrote of there having been 110 factories and 50,000 workers involved in work that directly supported the German war effort. These factories, the report claimed, included one that made aircraft components, another that produced poison gas, as well as others that produced optical goods, anti-aircraft and field guns, electrical gauges and X-ray apparatus. There was also a munitions storage depot and a barracks made up of wooden huts.

The report also included the fact that Dresden was a major military traffic road route, both north to south and east to west. Train-wise, a railway line linked with Berlin, Prague and Vienna, as well as the Munich-Breslau, and Hamburg-Leipzig lines. The obvious question has to be asked as to why Dresden, such a strategically important location for both road and rail movements, which linked directly to numerous other German cities and beyond, along with its large number of factories that produced goods for the German military war effort, was not targeted with Allied air attacks before January 1945.

Each of the RAF air crews that took part in the Dresden raid on the night of 13/14 February, were given a memo which read:

> Dresden, the seventh largest city in Germany and not much smaller than Manchester is also the largest unbombed built up area the enemy has got. In the midst of winter with refugees pouring westward and troops to be rested, roofs are at a premium, not only to give shelter to workers, refugees, and troops alike, but to house the administrative service displaced from other areas. At one time well known for its china, Dresden has developed into an industrial city of first class importance. The intentions of the attack are to hit the enemy where he will feel it most, behind an already partially collapsed front, and incidentally to show the Russians when they arrive, what Bomber Command can do.

The attack on Dresden was due to have been led by the USAAF Eighth Air Force, but due to bad weather over Europe, it was left to the RAF's Bomber Command to commence the raid. It was the Allies turn to put thought into their attacks. This came in the form of how the air strike on the city was carried out.

After the Pathfinder aircraft from No. 83 Squadron had dropped their magnesium parachute flares to light up the area to be attacked, the main bomber force took off from airfields in England at around 5.30pm, and made its way across the English Channel and across France towards Germany. Between them the 254 Lancaster bombers were carrying a total of 500 tons of high explosive bombs and 375 tons of incendiary devices. The high-explosive bombs weighed between 500lbs and 4,000lbs; each of them capable of causing extensive damage to the areas they landed on. The different types of bombs made up a potent cocktail once they detonated on the ground, the first caused the damage and an air corridor for the incendiary bombs to spread their flames far and wide.

The first bombs were dropped at almost 10.15pm, causing death and destruction, and whilst 'rescue' teams on the ground were still tending to damaged buildings and wounded civilians from the first attack, three hours later, at 1.20am on 15 February a second wave of US Flying fortresses dropped a further 770 tons of bombs on the already ruined city.

Once the raid was over, the flames and smoke from the subsequent fires could be seen some 60 miles away.

For those who survived the raids, it would be debatable as to whether they saw themselves as being lucky or victims, as they would have undoubtedly witnessed sights that would have haunted them for the rest of their lives. The question they would have no doubt been asking themselves was, why?

Once the news of the raids had made its way back to the UK, uncomfortable questions started to be asked as to why the bombings had taken place, that is, amongst politicians and the upper classes of society. The working classes cared less, probably seeing it as pay back for what they had to endure during the time of the Blitz, when the German Luftwaffe targeted London and other major British cities with their bombs.

There was little Germany could do in a physical sense to retaliate for the bombing of Dresden, so the best they could do was to leave their response to Joseph Goebbels, the Reich Minister of Propaganda for Nazi Germany. This was the man who was virulently anti-Semitic, and who advocated progressively harsher discrimination against Jews, including their extermination in the Holocaust. On 16 February, his Ministry issued a press release that stated there were no factories or other war-related industries in Dresden, and that it was nothing other than a city of culture. Nine days later Goebbels' Propaganda Ministry released a leaflet which included a photograph of the burnt bodies of two children. Under the heading, '*Dresden – Massacre of Refugees*', it claimed 200,000 Germans had been killed in the bombing raids.

On 4 March, a lengthy article appeared about the Dresden Bombings in the weekly Nazi newspaper *Das Reich*, which had been started by Goebbels. It bemoaned the fact that a cultural icon had been destroyed, and spoke of the suffering and destruction that the bombing had caused. It did not, however, make any mention about the problems it had undoubtedly caused them in a military sense, nor did it draw a comparison with the bombings that the Luftwaffe had carried out during the Blitz. Loathe him or like him, Goebbels was good at what he did.

Despite the information released by Nazi Germany in relation to Dresden having come from her Propaganda Ministry, Mr Richard Stokes, MC, Labour MP for Ipswich and an opponent of area bombing, brought the matter to the attention of the House of Commons. Mr Stokes had served during the First World War in the Royal Field Artillery, reaching the rank of major and being awarded the Military Cross.

There were those who questioned the purpose of such raids so late in the war, and matters weren't helped any when elements of the Press started referring to the Dresden attacks as 'terror bombings'.

Two days after the bombings, the matter had become so contentious that Air Commodore Colin McKay Grierson, of the Supreme Headquarters Allied Expeditionary Force, had to defend the actions at a hastily arranged Press conference.

> First of all, Dresden and other similar locations throughout Germany are the centres to which evacuees are being moved. They are centres of communication through which traffic is moving across to the Russian Front, and from the Western Front to the East, and they are sufficiently close to the Russian

Front for the Russians to continue the successful prosecution of their battle. I think these three reasons probably covered cover the bombing.

One of the journalists present at the briefing asked Grierson whether the principal aim of the bombing was to cause confusion amongst the refugees or to blast German communications which carried military supplies. Grierson answered that the primary aim of the air strike was to attack lines of communications to prevent the Germans from moving around military supplies, as well as manpower to and from any direction. Unfortunately Grierson then made an off-the-record comment along the lines of the raid also helping to destroy 'what is left of German morale'.

After the briefing, a war correspondent working for the Associated Press filed a story reporting that the Allies had resorted to terror bombing. Other newspapers picked up on the story, which in turn led to Major Stokes asking his questions in the House of Commons on 6 March 1945.

At this stage, Winston Churchill, who had instigated the raids, suddenly started to try and distance himself from the bad press that the raids had brought to him and his government. The only reason any of this took place was because of his pushing and determination to ensure they would happen.

Churchill, maybe because he realised where all of this was going to end up, sent a memo on 28 March 1945 to General Hastings Lionel Ismay, for the British Chiefs of Staff and the Chief of the Air Staff. The memo which appeared in the 2005 book, *Dresden* by Frederick Taylor and published by Bloomsbury, read as follows:

> It seems to me that the moment has come when the question of bombing of German cities simply for the sake of increasing the terror, though under other pretexts, should be reviewed. Otherwise we will come into control of utterly ruined land. The destruction of Dresden remains a serious query against the conduct of Allied bombing. I am of the opinion that military objectives must henceforward be more strictly studied in our own interests than that of the enemy.

> The Foreign Secretary has spoken to me on this subject, and I feel the need for more precise concentration upon military objectives such as oil and communications behind the immediate battle zone, rather than on mere acts of terror and wanton destruction, however impressive.

It was amazing how quickly Churchill appeared to have completely changed his attitude on the matter. The idea for the attack on Dresden was his plan to start with, it was he who was pushing for the raids to go ahead, so to now try and distance himself from the fallout of those raids did him no credit at all.

In direct contrast to Churchill's view on the matter was that of Air Chief Marshal Arthur 'Bomber' Harris, who having been shown a paraphrased version of what Churchill had said, wrote to the Ministry of Air. His words were recorded in the 1983 book by Norman Longmate, *The Bombers,* published by Hutchings & Company.

> I assume that the view under consideration is something like this: no doubt in the past we were justified in attacking German cities. But to do so was always repugnant and now that the Germans are beaten anyway we can properly abstain from proceeding with these attacks. This is a doctrine to which I could never subscribe. Attacks on cities like any other act of war are intolerable unless they are strategically justified. But they are strategically justified in so far as they tend to shorten the war and preserve the lives of Allied soldiers. To my mind we have absolutely no right to give them up unless it is certain that they will not have this effect. I do not personally regard the whole of the remaining cities of Germany as worth the bones of one British Grenadier.
>
> The feeling, such as there is, over Dresden, could be easily explained by any psychiatrist, it is connected with German bands and Dresden shepherdesses. Actually Dresden was a mass of munitions works, an intact government centre, and a key transportation point to the East. It is none of these things now.

Harris wasn't the only senior military man who vehemently disagreed with Churchill's memo. Under pressure from the Chiefs of Staff, and in keeping with Harris's response, Churchill withdrew his memo of 28 March and replaced it with a slightly different one.

> It seems to me that the moment has come when the question of the so called 'area bombing' of German cities should be reviewed from the point of view of our own interests. If we come into control of an entirely ruined land, there will be a great shortage of accommodation for ourselves and our allies. We must see to it that our attacks do no more harm to ourselves in the long run than they do to the enemy's war effort.

I can't actually decide if this is a case of Churchill simply not thinking about what he was saying before he actually said it, and then once he had time to reflect on what he had said, changed his words because it was the right thing to do, or whether his words were what he actually thought, and he only subsequently changed them if he was sufficiently challenged by others, or thought it would harm him politically if he didn't.

As the raids on Dresden were Churchill's idea in the first place, his change of heart, or what was more like a U-turn, was more than likely because of the combined political backlash in the House of Commons, along with the disdain for the attacks that had been written about in the Press.

In the immediate aftermath of the Second World War, the International War Crimes Trials took place, which for the European theatre of war, were held in the main at Nuremberg. There were no German military personnel put on trial specifically for the Luftwaffe's Blitz of London and other major cities during 1940. The offence many of the German hierarchy were charged with was waging aggressive war. If Britain and her Allies had lost the war, the likes of Churchill and Arthur Harris would have no doubt been put on trial for war crimes just for the part each of them played in the attacks on Dresden.

Dresden, it could be argued, was not one of Churchill's finest hours, but not so much for the actual attacks themselves, but in the manner in which he conducted himself in the aftermath. As Arthur Harris had so succinctly said, Britain and her Allies were at war with Germany, and if bombing Dresden and other German cities brought an end to war more quickly and just one British life was saved, then bombing any German city was something that Bomber Harris felt was a price worth paying.

After all, the British authorities had experienced first-hand the Luftwaffe's air raids on Coventry during 1940 and 1941, and the subsequent destruction of many of its finest buildings, along with the effects the bombings had on the city's people, 1,200 of whom were killed in the raids.

On 13 February 1945, the remaining Jewish residents of Dresden were ordered to report themselves for deportation on 16 February, but the Allied air raids on the city on 13 and 14 February overtook the intended deportations. Many of those due to hand themselves in to the city's authorities on 16 February were dead, having being killed in the air raids. For some of those who survived the chaos that followed, they managed to escape the clutches of the Gestapo, and survive the remaining few months of the war.

The Allied air raids on Dresden remain controversial to this very day. It is a topic that has been discussed time and time again by historians and other interested parties from many different countries.

If the eight-month Blitz on the British cities of London, Coventry, Liverpool, Birmingham, Glasgow, Plymouth, Bristol, Exeter, Portsmouth, Southampton, Hull, Manchester, Belfast, Sheffield, Newcastle, Nottingham and Cardiff had resulted in the Nazis winning the war, I somehow do not feel there would have been too many discussions taking place in Germany about the rights and wrongs of the more than 40,000 British civilians who were killed or died as a result of the raids and the tens of thousands of others who were injured. To Germany, it would have simply been the case that they were fighting a war, and they did what they did to win it. War is a dirty business, which results in thousands of innocent people dying and family homes being destroyed, but no nation fights a war to come second.

After the end of the First World War, the development of military aircraft moved forward at an alarming rate, both in fighters and bomber aircraft, and throughout the 1920s and 1930s there were military personnel from different countries, who were of a mindset that air forces could win wars, so saving the need for men to take to the seas and battlefields on land to fight each other. The thinking behind this was somewhat flawed as it was a principle based on not appreciating that bomber aircraft could be prevented from reaching their targets, by both fighter aircraft and anti-aircraft batteries. But the principle behind the idea was the same thinking that was considered during the Second World War, no doubt by both sides.

The thinking of the 1920s and 1930s saw the night-time bombing of enemy cities as a way of destroying industry, factories, government and communications, which if successfully carried out, deprived an enemy of waging war. The intentional bombing of civilian populations was seen as a way of causing a collapse in the civilian morale, as well as a loss in production of much-needed items for a nation's war effort.

The bombing of cities was always going to be contentious, because of the large civilian populations that lived within them. But the rule of thumb, and misplaced justification as to what was permissible and what constituted 'terror bombing', appears to have been if a country didn't actually target civilians, but in the efforts of attacking strategic military targets, killed them, it wasn't against the law. A somewhat warped sense of self-justification if ever I have heard one.

In 1956, the cities of Dresden and Coventry entered into a twinning relationship. Both cities were heavily bombed during the Second World War, with Dresden being bombed, in part as 'payback' for the bombing of Coventry. This showed that even through the worst of times, reconciliation was still possible.

Chapter 14

Malayan Emergency 1948

The Malayan Emergency, or the Anti-British National Liberation War, depending on which side was describing the conflict, lasted for more than twelve years between 16 June 1948 and 12 July 1960, and was a guerrilla war fought in the Federation of Malaya. In essence the warring factions were the Federation of Malaya, British and other Commonwealth forces who were up against the Malayan National Liberation Army, the military wing of the Malayan Communist Party.

Other than British and Malayan soldiers, countries that also sent troops to take part on the side of the Commonwealth included Southern Rhodesia, the Central African Federation, Fiji, Australia, New Zealand and Thailand.

The Second World War had been a bad time for Malaya in more ways than one. She had been occupied by the Japanese from late 1941, but despite having vast reserves of both rubber and tin, Malaya was only allowed to produce as much rubber as Japan needed for her own domestic purposes, which meant many of the tin mines became unused and derelict, whilst large numbers of rubber plantations were simply abandoned. Rice imports during this same period were almost non-existent, and as rice made up such a large part of the Malayan daily diet, many people simply struggled to survive.

There was a belief amongst many Malays that British troops would soon return, release them from their nightmare occupation by the Japanese, and that everything would be back to how it was before. British troops would return, but not for another three years, which for a number of Malays was too late, whilst for others there was a feeling of having been abandoned. Sadly, along with Singapore, Churchill and his wartime government had decided that winning the war in Europe was more important than rescuing the peoples of Malaya and Singapore.

With the Japanese surrender on 2 September 1945, Malaya was in a bad way, especially in an economic sense. Unemployment was high, food prices were highly inflated, what jobs were available offered relatively poor wages. The Malayan people were not happy, with the war over and the Japanese gone, they expected a lot more from Britain.

With the war finally at an end Britain tried to set up what they called a Malayan Union, which would make all citizens equal regardless of their ethnicity. This did not go down well with the nation's ethnic Malay population and they rejected the proposal. Things just went from bad to worse. Britain withdrew the proposal, which for many Chinese was the last straw, leaving them feeling badly let down for their wartime efforts against the Japanese.

Meanwhile, in the background, the Malayan Communist Party stepped up its anti-British propaganda, for which the British were providing them with plenty of ammunition to use against them. In a nutshell, that's how the build-up to the Malayan Emergency came about.

The incident that began the emergency took place at 8.30am on the morning of 16 June 1948, when three European rubber plantation managers, Arthur Walker, John Allison, and Ian Christian, were killed by three Chinese men.

Just two days later, on 18 June 1948, the British government enacted emergency powers into law, initially in the region of Perak (where the murder of the three plantation managers had taken place), before they were extended countrywide the following month. All left-wing parties, including the Malayan Communist Party, were made illegal, and the police were given sweeping powers to detain anybody who was, or whom they suspected of being, a communist. But Chin Peng, the Secretary General of the Malayan Communist Party, escaped capture and made his way to the country's more rural areas, where he formed the Malayan National Liberation Army, which was also known by other similar sounding names, in 1949. Peng began a guerrilla campaign, which mainly targeted the country's colonial resources, which in the main were the rubber plantations and the tin mines.

The first guerrilla act carried out by the Malayan National Liberation Army, was the attack and capture of the town of Gua Musang.

The Malayan National Liberation Army was basically the wartime Malayan Peoples Anti-Japanese army, which ironically had been trained by the British army, and had been disbanded in December 1945 and all weapons handed into the British military administration. Somewhere in the region of 4,000 members of the Malayan Peoples Anti-Japanese army held on to their weapons and went rogue.

Between 1946 and 1948, unrest amongst the Malayans continued which led to strikes, despite the fact that the British administration in Malaya was trying its best to get the economy back on track. Matters were not helped when it transpired that monies from the nation's tin and rubber industries were thought better spent propping up Britain's own post war economic recovery.

So by the time Winston Churchill, the Conservative MP for Woodford in Essex, and Party leader became prime minister for the second time on 25 October 1951, the problems in Malaya had already been going on for five years. The added difficulty for Churchill to have to deal with was his age and failing health. Just five weeks after becoming prime minister for a second time, he celebrated his seventy-seventh birthday, whilst only two years earlier, whilst on holiday in France, he had suffered a minor stroke. His declining health had become so noticeable that by December 1951, King George VI had considered asking him to step down, but with the king dying in February 1952, and the fact that Churchill remained in office until 1955, it is highly unlikely that he ever had the opportunity to do so.

The Malayan National Liberation Army consisted in the main of some 500,000 ethnic Chinese. The Chinese population supported the MNLA mainly because of the isolation the more than 3 million ethnic Chinese, who lived in Malaya, felt in having no land rights or the right to vote in elections. The guerrilla fighters were well organised, well fed, and well supported by large numbers of the general population, which they needed to be. They were also an excellent source of much-needed intelligence and information.

It was ironic that the very men whom the British had trained to fight against the Japanese, were now fighting against them in support of communism.

On 6 October 1951, just prior to Churchill becoming prime minister, the British High Commissioner in Malaya, Sir Henry Gurney, was assassinated in an ambush in the Pahang province, Malaya, by members of the Malayan Communist Party. The Communist leader, Chin Peng, later announced that the ambush in which Sir Henry was killed, was just routine and not a targeted ambush. They had no idea who was in the vehicle and only knew of the High Commissioner's death when they heard about it from news reports.

Churchill's choice as Malaya's next High Commissioner was General Gerald Templer in January 1952, who was given the direction in which the government wished to follow in relation to Malaya, by the Secretary of State for the Colonies.

Templer was an experienced man who had fought in both the First and Second World wars and whose father had held the rank of Lieutenant Colonel with the Royal Irish Fusiliers.

On 27 February 1952, there was a discussion in the House of Lords about the situation in Malaya, the motion for which had been put by Lord Ogmore of Bridgend with the intention of ascertaining the government's plans and intentions in relation to Malaya. What Lord Ogmore was asking, was now that General Templer had been given the 'direction' in which the government wanted him to go, how was that work to be implemented?

Lord Ogmore had worries and concerns about what was actually happening in Malaya, as resignations in the country had become commonplace, with the head of the Malaya Police Mr Gray quitting, along with the man in charge of the country's CID. The chief secretary for Malaya also left his position, as did General Harold Briggs, who had been Director of Operations, Malaya, between 1950 and 1951.

The real question here, and one which went a long way to understanding which way Churchill and the Conservative Party intending taking the situation in Malaya, was did they see the situation as being a military one or a political one? That decision would ultimately have a massive effect on the peoples of both Malaya and Singapore.

Churchill was a man of war, of that there was no doubt, he had proved it numerous times over the years. The question now was in which direction would he go in Malaya? He was nothing if predictable, he chose to take direct military action against the communist rebels who were trying to take control of the country, as the way of best dealing with the Malaya Emergency. This was endorsed with his selection of General Templer as the British High Commissioner in Malaya.

Although there was concern in certain circles about Churchill's decision as how best to deal with Malaya, Templer did make inroads into dealing with the situation. What was implemented was a 'hearts and minds' strategy in an effort to win over the population and in doing so, distance them from supporting the insurgent rebels. When an army is fighting against an enemy army, everything is clear, there are defined lines and fighting is usually out in the open. But when an army is fighting against an undefined guerrilla force the rules of engagement are completely different. It is the guerrillas who usually have the upper hand, because they can utilise the terrain they are fighting in much better than an attacking army, so fighting them head on, in a military sense, is not always the best tactic. America found that out for itself with the war in Vietnam.

What isn't clear is whether Templer was implementing what he had been directed to do by Churchill and the Conservative Party, or whether the 'hearts and minds' policy was his own idea, or that of Robert Thompson, who was the Permanent Secretary of Defence for Malaya and worked closely with Templer. Despite having some 40,000 British and Commonwealth troops stationed in Malaya, the decision was taken to pursue the policy of 'hearts and minds'. The tactic of building and policing fortified villages to protect the local population from the unwanted attention, threats and reprisals of the rebels proved particularly successful. The safety people enjoyed from this new way of life made them less likely to want to support the rebels, whilst at the same time making them more likely to productively engage with the British authorities. Templer also proposed the idea of granting Malayan citizenship to more than 2.5 million non-Malayan people who were living in the country, over a million of whom were ethnic Chinese. He also initiated a scheme that offered rewards and incentives to rebels and their families if they surrendered and gave up their struggle.

Templer, talking about the situation in Malaya, said, 'The answer lies not in pouring more troops into the jungle, but in the hearts and minds of the people.'

When Templer left Malaya in 1954, the situation had noticeably improved, but it was a long way from being over. The Malaya Emergency, which had been declared on 16 June 1948, was finally declared to be over by the government of Malaya on 12 July 1960, but the troubles in the country didn't fully come to an end until 1989.

I suppose the real question here is whether, with his age and failing health, Churchill should have even been the leader of the Conservative

Party, let alone the country's prime minister. The added stress that would have placed on his physical being would have been immense. Whether this combination affected his decision making process, we shall never know.

Since Winston Churchill, and up to and including Boris Johnson, there have been fourteen prime ministers of the United Kingdom. Of these the six eldest when they took office, are listed below.

Anthony Eden was 57 when he took office in 1955. Harold Macmillan was 63 when he took office in 1957. Alec Douglas-Home was 60 when he took office in 1963. Harold Wilson was 58 when he took office in 1974, James Callaghan was 64 when he took office in 1976 and Theresa May was 59 when she became prime minister in 2016.

Chapter 15

Mau Mau Uprising 1952

In the case of the Mau Mau Uprising I do not believe that it was a case of bad judgement on Churchill's part for actual decisions that he did or didn't make, after all, it was an ongoing situation that he and his party had inherited, in so far as there had been problems in Kenya since the British had taken control of the country in 1920. I believe that he was not physically fit enough to be running the country in 1951, and should not have been in a position to have become prime minister, that was where his judgement was in question. After his minor stroke in 1949 he should have known it was time for him to retire. That he didn't, I feel was for two reasons. Firstly, his desire to be of service to his country, and the British Empire which was very dear to him, along with a need to be 'on the front line', where the action was, where he had been for most of his adult life. Ultimately, I feel it was these two personal needs that he allowed to override what he quite possibly knew was the right thing to do: to stand aside and step down. The motivators of being in control and having power, especially when they have been part of you for your entire life, are very difficult to let go of. I believe this was the case with Churchill. Knowing that his country had called upon him again to lead them through difficult times was something that he could neither ignore nor refuse to do. That was the calibre of the man.

Kenya became part of the British Empire in 1920 and remained so until it gained independence in 1963. But peace and harmony were not two words that could be used to describe the relationship between the Kenyans and the British colonists. Finally, after thirty years of being a British Colony the Kenya Land and Freedom Army (KLFA), who were also known as the Mau Mau, rose up against their British masters, in what became known as the Mau Mau Uprising or Rebellion.

On 20 October 1952, a year less one day from when Winston Churchill had become prime minister for the second time, the Governor of Kenya, Evelyn Baring, signed an order declaring a State of Emergency. Churchill was soon to be celebrating his seventy-eighth birthday, and having to deal with this situation couldn't have come at a worse time, as he was already actively engaged in dealing with the problems of the Malaya Emergency. It would have been difficult enough for a younger man having to deal with two such heavyweight political incidents simultaneously being played out on the world stage, but for the ageing Churchill, just two years away from his eightieth birthday, the pressure must have been immense.

Just eight months after the signing of the state of emergency in Kenya, and with the ongoing problems Churchill was having in Malaya, his health took a turn for the worse when he had a stroke, just after dinner on the evening of 23 June 1953, at No. 10 Downing Street. This time it was more serious than the one he had in 1949, and reportedly left him paralysed down his entire left side, but rather than being hospitalised or taking to his bed, he was, somewhat remarkably, back at work at a cabinet meeting the following morning, acting as if nothing had happened. It is reported that nobody present that morning realised that there was anything wrong with him. His condition deteriorated and became so bad that he wasn't expected to make it beyond the weekend. News of what had actually happened had been kept from the public as well as his colleagues in Parliament. The story was that he was suffering from exhaustion and was taking a period of time out so that he could fully recover, and would be staying at his country home to recuperate. Just over three months later, in October 1953, he was back to work, full time, making his return at that year's Conservative Party conference held at Margate in Kent.

Most people in a similar situation, and at 79 years old, would I believe, have retired, but not Churchill, doggedly he hung on to power. Was that because he needed to, because it was what kept him going, and without it he was concerned that might be the end of him? He finally retired on 5 April 1955, aged 80.

Baring's predecessor as Governor of Kenya had been Philip Mitchell, who had held the post between 1944 and 1952. Sadly, it would appear that he had not been as effective as he could and should have been, there were even suggestions that Mitchell had resorted to turning a blind eye to a lot of the Mau Mau activity throughout the country, but fortunately for

Churchill and his government, they were being kept up to date with the full extent of what had really been going on by Acting Governor, Henry Potter, who in turn had been informing Oliver Lyttelton, the Colonial Secretary, in London.

When Baring became the governor of Kenya on 30 September 1952, nobody, including the Colonial Office in London, made him fully aware of what he was stepping into, which is not only unforgivable, it beggars belief. Was there a hidden agenda that meant it had already been decided that Baring was deemed to be a suitable individual to take the blame if things did eventually go badly wrong in Kenya?

On 21 October 1952, the morning after the state of the emergency had been declared, Operation Jock Scott was put into place, which suggested it had been prepared well in advance of the announcement of the state of emergency. The British army carried out the arrests of 181 Mau Mau leaders throughout the city of Nairobi, one of whom was Jomo Kenyatta, an anti-colonial activist, who went on to become the country's prime minister and president.

News of the operation was believed to have been leaked as there were many others who the authorities had gone to arrest, but who had already made good their escape.

The day after the operation, the prominent loyalist chief, Nderi, was discovered having been brutally hacked to death. Over the following months a number of other violent murders took place, some of which were against white settlers, but despite a 'strong' response to such events rather than making the local population safer, the British simply alienated themselves by their actions, which made it very easy for the Mau Mau to win over any wavering tribesmen.

To try and prevent any further murders by the Mau Mau, three battalions of the King's African Rifles were recalled to the country, and to help stem the tide of fear felt by white settler communities, one battalion of the Lancashire Fusiliers, which had been stationed in Egypt, was flown into the country

The situation in Kenya showed just how little the British establishment had learnt over the years, in relation to underestimating an enemy in a military sense. The problems which came to a head in Kenya in 1952 with the declaration of a state of emergency, was a culmination of Mau Mau violence going back to the early years of Britain taking control of

Kenya in 1920. But nothing had ever really been taken that seriously, as militarily they were not seen as being a real threat. It was the same old story of British arrogance being the controlling factor in such matters.

When Churchill retired from office in 1955, the problems in Kenya with the Mau Mau were still apparent, so he and his administration had not been able to bring the dispute to an end. Nor would Anthony Eden for that matter, who took over from Churchill as prime minister. It was 1960 before the uprising was fully suppressed and under control, under the leadership of Harold Macmillan.

Chapter 16

Other Bits about Churchill

As I delved into Winston Churchill's life, I found that a raft of interesting information slowly appeared about him, but each story on its own would never be enough to fill up a chapter's worth of information in a book. However, all put together they do.

I'll start with claims that Churchill was a racist, which have been made several times over the years. To evidence this allegation, his past comments, views, beliefs, and writings are trolled through, to find appropriate quotes that are then used against him. The question is, was he a racist? Let's look at some of those allegations.

Earlier in the book I wrote about how the language used at the beginning of the twentieth century was very different to what it is today. I made mention of him being an imperialist and how he felt that a white man was superior, but I don't see how that qualifies him as being a racist. By believing that the white man was superior he never said that it was permissible to treat a non-white person in a disingenuous or brutal manner. In fact, according to John Charmley in his book, *Churchill: The End of Glory*, he even ranked white Protestant Christians above white Catholics. Is that racism?

The first recorded use of the word racism came about in 1902, when an American Union soldier named Richard Henry Pratt was speaking against the evils of racial segregation, in relation to Native American Red Indians, when he said the following:

> Segregating any class or race of people apart from the rest of the people, kills the progress of the segregated people or makes their growth very slow. Association of races and classes is necessary to destroy racism and classism.

This was the same era that Churchill grew up in. In 1902, Churchill was 28 years old, and Native American Red Indians lost their lands because they were a lesser developed culture, not because of the colour of their skin.

Churchill did not think well of Gandhi but not necessarily because he was Indian but because he was advocating self-determination for India, which if forthcoming, could damage the British Empire in which Churchill so vehemently believed. Perhaps it follows that if Churchill saw white Christian Protestants as being 'top of the tree', how would he have viewed the world with a reduced British Empire, or no Empire at all. He would have had to rethink his entire values and views on everything he had spent his entire life believing in.

He spoke poorly of Gandhi, but maybe that was because he saw him being a real threat to everything he believed in. To Churchill, it didn't matter that Britain had taken India for her own benefit and financial gain, to him it was British India and certainly not to be given up to anybody.

Here are just some of the quotes Churchill made in relation to Gandhi.

> It is alarming and nauseating to see Mr Gandhi, a seditious Middle Temple lawyer, now posing as a fakir, striding half naked up the steps of the Vice-Regal Palace.

Although Gandhi was clearly not an individual who Churchill liked, I believe that comment is one of class rather than anything to do with racism.

> Gandhi should not be released on the account of a mere threat of fasting. We should be rid of a dead man and an enemy of the Empire if he died.

An article on the BBC website in 2015 and a similar one in the *Daily Telegraph* newspaper in 2012, in relation to Churchill's attitude towards Jewish people, talked about how in 2012 a proposed 'Churchill Centre' in Jerusalem was objected to by some, including one comment that said, 'He is no stranger to the latent anti-Semitism of his generation and class.'

I feel that is a somewhat unfair and ill-thought-out comparison to make. To say that of Churchill, does that not mean that everybody of his generation and class were also culpable, and by his generation does that mean everybody of his class who lived between 30 November 1874 and 24 January 1965? Should the same generalisation be made of King George VI, Neville Chamberlain, Clement Atlee, Anthony Eden, and David Lloyd George, who were of the same generation and class as Churchill?

In 1899, Winston Churchill had a book published entitled *The River War*, which was about his wartime experiences fighting against Mahdist forces in the Sudan.

The Mahdist War had begun in 1881 and finally ended in 1899, and the book was written as a specific reference, and from a very personal perspective about the Mahdists of Sudan at that time. The following is a small snippet from the book.

> How dreadful are the curses which Mohammedanism lays on its votaries! Besides the fanatical frenzy, which is as dangerous in a man as hydrophobia in a dog, there is this fearful fatalistic apathy.

> Improvident habits, slovenly systems of agriculture, sluggish methods of commerce and insecurity of property exist wherever the followers of the Prophet rule or live.

No offence is intended to anybody by repeating the above words, as there is a specific purpose for me doing so. On 26 April 2014, Paul Weston, who at the time was the leader of the Far Right political party, Liberty Great Britain, which had been registered with the Electoral Commission in 2013, was arrested on the steps of Winchester Guildhall for failing to comply with a dispersal notice issued under section 27 of the Violent Crime Reduction Act 2006 as he was reading out a passage from the aforementioned book, which was critical of Islam. He had been reported to the police by a member of the public after they had asked him if he had permission to give the speech and he replied that he did not. At the police station Weston was then re-arrested for a racially aggravated public order offence under section 4 of the Public Order Act 1986, compounded with a Crime and Disorder Act 1998 section 31 racially aggravated public order offence, and was bailed to return to Winchester Police on 24 May.

This book makes no comment on what were or what might have been Mr Weston's reasons for quoting from Winston Churchill's book, as this book is about Winston Churchill and not Mr Weston, but I use it as an example of just how powerful words can be, and how over time they can possibly become even more powerful than they were ever first intended. However, I believe there is a subtle difference in this case. Churchill made his comments in 1899, and they were aimed at a specific small group of individuals who he had fought against in a war; his words and comments were not, I would suggest, intended to describe an entire religious group. I am sure that he had absolutely no thought that 115 years after those same words had been happily accepted for publication in a book, which was widely read, they would be repeated with any intent to cause religious offence.

The fact that Churchill's comments were published in a book, I would respectfully suggest, show that his views were more than likely commonplace at the time when Britain did not have as diverse a religious society as it does today.

Personally, I do not believe Churchill was a racist, but I fully accept that it is quite simple for individuals to hold up words that he once spoke so far back, and claim that by today's standards they are racist views.

The siege of Sidney Street, which took place in January 1911 in the East End of London, showed another side of Churchill that highlighted the claims that he was a bit of a show off and an individual who was always spoiling for a 'bit of a fight'.

There had been a combination of events starting with an attempted jewellery robbery at Houndsditch in the City of London. Those responsible were a gang of Latvian immigrants. But this was no ordinary robbery, because it resulted in three policemen being killed by the gang, a further two being wounded, and the leader of the Latvian gang, George Gardstein, was also killed. Ironically he hadn't been killed by the police but by another gang member, who had blasted away at the police and accidentally shot him in the back. His body was found the following day in a property where he had rented a room.

The Latvian gang had broken into a jeweller's shop at 11 Exchange Buildings in Houndsditch, at around 10pm on 16 December 1910, by tunnelling in from the unoccupied premises next door, and were heard by a neighbour, Max Weil, who informed passing police officer, Constable

Piper, who was walking his beat. He then calmly knocked on the door of the premises and spoke with a gentleman who answered. Piper was immediately suspicious of the man, but not wanting to arouse any concern, he made good his excuses and left. On his way to Houndsditch he bumped into two other constables, Choate and Woodhams, and asked them to go and keep observation on the premises whilst he went to get more help from Bishopsgate police station. Remember that this was a time long before the police used radios to contact each other.

By 11.30pm, several police officers had arrived at the scene. It was soon after that the Latvian gang, realising they had been rumbled, decided to shoot their way out, in their efforts to escape capture. In doing so they killed the three police officers from the City of London Police, Sergeants Charles Tucker and Robert Bentley, along with Constable Walter Choate and wounding a further two. Choate was reportedly shot twelve times, but remarkably wasn't killed instantly. He was taken to the London Hospital in Whitechapel Road, where he was operated on but died at 5.30am the following morning.

For some reason, rumours spread that those responsible for the attempted robbery and the death of the policemen were Jewish. To quash any such rumours that this was the case, which it wasn't, the coroner took the unusual step of publicly announcing that the dead man was uncircumcised.

The matter was jointly investigated by the Metropolitan and City of London police forces, and within a couple of weeks all but two of the Latvian gang had been identified and arrested. Information was received that the final two members of the gang were hiding at 100 Sidney Street, in Stepney, East London. On the evening of 2 January 1911, a combination of armed police officers from the Metropolitan and City of London forces rushed to the scene before the two Latvians could escape.

After the two men realised they had been discovered, they opened fire, the police surrounded the premises, and a siege began which lasted for more than six hours, with both sides repeatedly firing upon each other. Tucked away in the middle of the police ranks, but extremely close to the action was the British Home Secretary, Winston Churchill, who had not only attended the scene himself, but authorised the deployment of the army, and very soon members of the Scots Guards, stationed at the

Tower of London, arrived on the scene along with soldiers from the Royal Engineers and the Royal Horse Artillery.

Fortuitously for Churchill there were newsreel cameras and photographers present, and in at least one photograph he can be seen looking away from the action and directly into the lens of a camera, the unknown photographer behind it, no doubt keenly aware of his identity. This was the first time such an incident had been recorded on film.

The siege ended at about 2.30pm when the building which the two Latvians were held up in, caught fire. How, or who was responsible is unclear. One of the two men had been shot before the fire took hold, and the body of the other man was found in the burnt-out ruins of the building. It is alleged that Churchill refused to allow the fire brigade to try and extinguish the flames, until no more firing could be heard coming from within the building.

A memorial service took place on 23 December 1910, at St Paul's Cathedral in the City of London, for the three murdered police officers. It was a bitterly cold day with fresh snow on the ground. Edward Wallington, a representative of King George V, the Lord Mayor of London, along with Winston Churchill, in his capacity as the Home Secretary, attended.

Churchill's fellow politicians were not impressed by his actions at Sidney Street, and the Conservative leader, Arthur Balfour, asked, 'I understand what the photographer was doing, but what was the right honourable gentleman doing?'

Churchill's detractors were quick to remark that his involvement at Sidney Street was an example of his lack of judgement and rashness, which was certainly not becoming of a man in his position.

It really was poor judgement on Churchill's part to go to Sidney Street during the siege. With literally hundreds of police officers on duty, many of whom were armed, his decision to authorise the army to attend and assist in the siege was questionable. His decision to prevent the fire brigade from dousing the flames at Sidney Street could be interpreted in two ways. Either he was trying to protect the wellbeing of the firemen, or he wanted to ensure that those inside the premises were dead.

Eight people were put on trial in relation to the attempted burglary at 11 Exchange Buildings. Only one person was found guilty, and that conviction was overturned on appeal.

Lord Halifax, who at the beginning of the Second World War had been the Secretary of State for Foreign Affairs, was somewhat of an interesting character. During the First World War, between November 1917 and December 1918, he was a major in the British army serving as the deputy director of labour supply at the Ministry of National Service. Initially he had been supportive of Lord Lansdowne's suggestion for a compromise peace with Germany. Halifax also had a major part in the Second World War. He was the foreign secretary in Neville Chamberlain's government at the outbreak of the war.

Chamberlain resigned as prime minister on the afternoon of 10 May 1940, a prerequisite of senior Labour officials agreeing to serve in a coalition government, after Chamberlain and his government only just survived a vote of no confidence, as a result of the deteriorating situation in Norway. There were different names placed 'in the hat' as to who should become the next prime minister, but these varied depending on which political party had put them forward. It has to be said at this stage, Churchill did not hold a particularly strong political position at the time and was certainly not the favourite to take over from Chamberlain. Two things appeared to have been going in his favour: firstly, it was his stance throughout the 1930s, of being against appeasing Hitler and the Nazi Party; and secondly, despite favouring Halifax for the role, Chamberlain suggested to King George VI that he ask Churchill to form a new government.

The person who everybody seemed to want to be the next prime minister, was Halifax: that was everybody other than Halifax himself. Chamberlain preferred Halifax, but possibly knowing the fight that was ahead, knew that Churchill was the better equipped individual to replace him. Archibald Sinclair, leader of the Liberal Party, wanted Halifax. The House of Lords wanted Halifax, the Labour Party wanted Halifax, even the king, who was no great lover of Churchill, wanted Halifax. It was even said that Churchill had agreed to serve under Halifax.

But Halifax to his credit was nothing if not honest. The entry in his diary for 9 May 1940 read as follows.

> I have no doubt at all in my own mind that for me to succeed him (Chamberlain) would create a quite impossible situation. Apart altogether from Churchill's qualities as compared with my own at this particular juncture, what would in fact be my

position? Churchill would be running defence, and in this connection, one could not fail to remember the relationship between Asquith and Lloyd George had broken down in the first war … I should speedily become a more or less honorary Prime Minister, living in a kind of twilight just outside the things that really mattered.

So it was that Churchill became the British prime minister on 10 May 1940. He certainly started off on the right foot. One of his first actions was to form a new War Cabinet. Two members of which were the ousted Chamberlain and Halifax.

Just two weeks after taking office, Churchill had to deal with his first main wartime crisis which was the evacuation of Belgian, British and French troops from Dunkirk. A test he passed with flying colours and a decision which probably resulted in Britain and her Allies winning the Second World War, because if the more than 300,000 allied troops had been killed or captured at Dunkirk, that would have been the war over, there and then.

An interesting footnote in relation to Churchill was that he was never awarded the Nobel Peace Prize for his part in fighting against, and bringing to an end, the tyranny of Nazism during the Second World War, but 8 years after the end of the war, he was eventually awarded a Nobel Peace Prize, but for literature. In writing his memoirs of the Second World War, the judging panel decided Churchill was worthy of the prize, 'for his mastery of historical and biographical descriptions as well as for brilliant oratory in defending exalted human values'. There were the souls of at least 3 million dead Indians who wouldn't readily agree with the last four words of that sentence.

Chapter 17

Churchill Imperialist or Racist?

I have decided to include this chapter in the book, despite the subject matter not actually been a flaw or error of judgement by Churchill. But as there are some who claim he was a racist, I think looking at the topic in more detail and from a wider perspective has some value and provides a more balanced viewpoint.

In today's society the subject of racism can be an uncomfortable and difficult topic to talk about, especially when history, regardless of how far back in time we go, is looked at through today's eyes and standards. By way of example, between 1972 and 1976 there was a TV programme entitled *Love Thy Neighbour,* about a white working-class socialist and his wife, played by Jack Smethurst and Kate Williams, who had a black couple, played by Rudolph Walker and Nina Baden-Semper, move in next door to them. Whilst the wives got on famously, the husbands clashed repeatedly, with the white character often coming off worse in verbal exchanges as well as often being made to look ignorant and bigoted. The series spawned a film of the same name, which first aired in 1973.

Although one of the most popular TV series of its time, it has never been repeated on television as by many of today's generation it is perceived as being racist.

The reason I give the above example is that a couple of comments that Churchill made, the first in 1919 and the latter in 1937, have been used by some observers to claim he was a racist. Personally, I don't believe that he was, and without trying to justify his words, it would be fair to say that his views and comments were held by others at the time that he made them. It feels quite strange having just written this paragraph, because I suddenly feel very conscious that if I do not condemn him for what he said, then there will be those who just assume that I hold similar views, which I don't.

In 1919, when he was the Secretary of State for War and the Secretary of State for Air, he had written a memo about the use of chemical weapons in war. In it he wrote.

> I cannot understand this squeamishness about the use of gas. I am strongly in favour of using poisoned gas against uncivilised tribes. The moral effect should be so good that the loss of life should be so good that the loss of life should be reduced to a minimum. It is not necessary to use only the most deadly gases: gases can be used which cause great inconvenience and would spread a lively terror and yet would leave no serious permanent effect on most of those affected.

Churchill was talking about its use during the First World War and in a military sense, but his memo is slightly confusing as it begins with him talking about being in favour of using poison gas against uncivilised tribes, and then he goes on to talk about using a gas that would leave no serious permanent effects, which sounds more like a reference to similar gases used by some police forces in instances of major public order.

Move forward to 1937 when he was the MP for Epping, he was addressing the Palestine Royal Commission:

> I do not admit for instance that a great wrong has been done to the Red Indians of America or the black people of Australia. I do not admit that a wrong has been done to these people by the fact that a stronger race, a higher grade race, a more worldly race to put it that way, has come in and taken their place.

I believe that these comments of Churchill's don't show what amounts to any form of racism, but rather imperialism, especially as Churchill was unashamedly an imperialist. But as Aborigines were the original peoples who occupied Australia, and Red Indians were the original occupants of America, I am not sure how he could say he does not feel that a great wrong had not been done to them, when they had their lands taken away from them by other nations who were just more advanced than they were.

Where I think Churchill suffers, maybe somewhat unfairly, is on the issue of being an imperialist. He wasn't alone: many at the time held similar views. The claim of racism against him is one that has come about in more recent times, but which is directly connected to his views and opinions as an imperialist as far back as the early 1900s. This is also a case of judging a historical figure by today's standards, which I don't think is a fair equation.

The British Empire, and alongside it, imperialism, began way back in 1583, when Sir Humphrey Gilbert, an MP, a soldier, an adventurer and an explorer, formally claimed the island of Newfoundland, located off of the east coast of North America. This later became referred to as the 'First' British Empire, and continued on until 1783. During this time, parts of the land masses of America and Africa became part of the British Empire, along with an extremely lucrative slave trade.

In the early 1600s, Britain became rivals with Holland to tap into the lucrative Asian spice trade that had previously been a Portuguese monopoly. Over time the spice trade was overtaken by the more profitable textiles industry.

The American Revolution, which also included the American Revolutionary War between 1775 and 1783, took place between 1765 and 1783. The result of this was a British defeat which saw American Independence as a result of the Peace of Paris in 1783.

The 'Second' British Empire ran for the relatively short period between 1783 and 1815, and included explorations throughout the Pacific region, a war with France under the leadership of Napoleon Bonaparte, and the abolition of slavery in 1807.

The Empire continued through both the First and Second World Wars, but in 1980, when Southern Rhodesia became the independent nation of Zimbabwe, it was the end of British colonisation of Africa. Britain's empire finally came to an end in 1997, when Hong Kong was returned to Chinese control.

Winston Churchill lived and died knowing nothing other than a British Empire which he wholeheartedly believed in. He was a man of his time, so being an imperialist was as normal to him as breathing air. His view of imperialism is that it benefited the people of the nations who were part of the British Empire. How much in the way of actual truth can be attached to that assumption, is unclear. It could be easily argued that an individual's wellbeing was the last thing on the mind of those who had claimed the lands of these other nations in the first place. The only concern then was 'what is in it for us'. The answer to that was such items as gold, rubber, oil, spices, tobacco and the like. The British Empire became very rich by plundering the natural resources of other countries.

Churchill believed that nations which Britain conquered and made part of her Empire, improved on all levels, and were far better off for having been conquered. This was regardless of what the conquered nation felt about the situation.

At a Cabinet meeting in 1921, Churchill's imperialism came to the fore during a discussion concerning the Chinese territory of Weihaiwei, which had been leased to the British in 1898. The lease was due to expire in 1930. The discussion in question was whether or not to return the territory to China before the due date. Churchill was almost incandescent. He comprehensively opposed the suggestion, stating that he for one was against the idea, no matter how worthless the territory in question might be. He made mention of how quickly Britain was willing to barter away such locations as Java and Corfu. His next comment showed how imperialism was the very blood of his veins. He stated, 'Why melt down the capital collected by our forebears to please a lot of pacifists.' The fact that the territories were simply being returned to their rightful owners, the relatives of the very same people they were taken from, was totally lost on Churchill.

He was such a deep-rooted imperialist, he simply could not comprehend returning the power of self-rule to the very people to whom the country belonged. A point that needs highlighting at this juncture is that Churchill grew up in a different world to most, and as a man the social classes he moved about in were the upper classes and the aristocracy. One of the norms of his social class in society was a belief in the racial superiority of the British, a belief that he adhered to as did many others. It crossed over political lines as well, and wasn't a belief held by just one particular political party.

During his second term as prime minister in 1952, Churchill told Lord Moran, his private physician:

> When you learn to think of a race as inferior beings it is difficult to get rid of that way of thinking. When I was a subaltern in India the Indians did not seem to be equal to the white man.

The above is from Paul Addison's book, first published in 1980, *The Political Beliefs of Winston Churchill.*

Conclusion

I am going to start with the positives. I believe that without Winston Churchill, Britain would have lost the Second World War. Of that I have absolutely no doubt.

He was the right man to lead the nation to victory during the Second World War, and I believe that he was the only man capable of delivering such an outcome. When Chamberlain decided it was time for him to resign in May 1940, there could not have been a better man waiting to take over, even though he wasn't the automatic choice, or anywhere near being the favourite to do so. Everyone wanted Lord Halifax to be become prime minister, including King George VI, the only person who didn't want him to get the job was Lord Halifax himself. Even he knew that Churchill was the best man for the job. Cometh the hour, cometh the man, cometh Winston Churchill.

If Chamberlain had stayed in power, it would have been debatable how much longer Britain would have managed to stave off defeat. America didn't come into the war until 7 December 1941, when Japan carried out her audacious attack on the American fleet at Pearl Harbor in Hawaii. The US didn't declare war on Germany until four days later on 11 December 1941.

Just two weeks after taking over as prime minister, Churchill came up with the idea of the 'small boats' rescue at Dunkirk. If anybody other than Churchill had been in charge at the time, I believe that would have been Britain out of the war, as over 300,000 of our men would have been killed or captured on the beaches of Dunkirk.

Winston Churchill had a bee in his bonnet about having daily meetings at 5pm, much to the annoyance of his military leaders. The Chief of the Imperial General Staff, Sir William Ironside, in particular found him annoying and frustrating in equal measures. He most definitely wasn't a fan of Churchill's, describing him as a 'desperate man who seemed to be more of a liability than an asset', a view that was shared by other senior military figures. Part of Ironside's frustration was borne out of the fact he had the impression that Churchill appeared to believe this was the way to do business in a military sense, which it wasn't.

Churchill was 65 when he became prime minister, an age at which most men would have been happily putting their feet up, warming their slippers in front of the fire and lighting up their pipe. Churchill had been waiting for this opportunity nearly all of his adult life, and he wasn't prepared to let it pass him by. When the opportunity arose, he grabbed it with both hands.

He was a very intelligent, articulate and driven individual. He had been a soldier, politician, author and journalist during his lifetime. Having said that, he was also a very complex individual.

As can be seen by reading through the pages of this book, some of his decisions were debatable, some were just out and out wrong and some of them cost many young men their lives. What is remarkable about him is that he didn't seem to learn his lesson when it came to which battles and campaigns to fight, but when it came to covering up errors, he would willingly do so especially if it meant that by disclosing such matters, they would reflect badly on him and his reputation.

He wasn't good at taking advice and could easily become quite entrenched in his views and opinions. It was almost if he allowed himself to be swayed on a particular matter, no matter how sensible an opinion or suggestion might be, it somehow translated into him being weak if he was seen to change his mind.

He liked to be where the action was whether that was in a political or military sense, or even in the unfolding events in Sidney Street in London, before the First World War.

He was a man of his time, his generation, and his class. He was not a racist, he was an imperialist, a man of the empire, who had never known a time without a British Empire., He believed that white Christian Protestants were 'top of the tree', but not to the detriment of people of different religions, cultures, or people of a different skin colour.

I don't believe that he was a man of the people, as in the working classes. How could he be? His family was aristocratic; he had been born into wealth where everything a person could want was provided, whether that was money, food, clothes, a home and a good education. He never knew poverty or a lack of food.

When he lost the general election in May 1945, Churchill was shocked. He couldn't believe it. He felt let down and betrayed by the very people, the working classes, who he felt owed him a debt of gratitude for winning the war and saving them from a lifetime of Nazi-enslavement as a member of the German Third Reich. He just didn't get it. He was needed by a grateful nation to win the war, but the general public didn't want things to return to how they had been before the war, which they believed Churchill did. Under Clement Atlee and the Labour Party, people saw the introduction of the National Health Service and improvements in the Welfare State, all of which was relevant to them as it affected their everyday lives.

Personally, I would like to say thank you to Winston Churchill, for the life that I am living. If he hadn't driven Britain, other Commonwealth countries, and our Allies on to a great victory, and the war had continued, my father might have been one of the soldiers who did not survive and I would not have been born.

Sources

Addison, Paul, *The Political Beliefs of Winston Churchill* (1980)

Longman, Norman, *The Bombers* (1983)

Taylor, Frederick, *Dresden* (2005)

Wikipedia

www.britishnewspaperarchive.co.uk

www.winstonchurchill.com

www.dailymail.co.uk

www.eyewitnesstohistory.com

www.nationalarchives.gov.uk

www.sport-leisure.blurtit.com

www.britannica.com

www.theguardian.com

www.cwgc.com

About the Author

Stephen is a happily retired police officer having served with Essex police as a constable for thirty years between 1983 and 2013. He is married to Tanya who is also his best friend.

Both his sons, Luke and Ross, were members of the armed forces, collectively serving five tours of Afghanistan between 2008 and 2013. Both were injured on their first tour. This led to Stephen's first book, *Two Sons in a Warzone – Afghanistan: The True Story of a Father's Conflict*, which was published in October 2010.

Both of his grandfathers served in and survived the First World War, one with the Royal Irish Rifles, the other in the Mercantile Navy, whilst his father was a member of the Royal Army Ordnance Corps during the Second World War.

Stephen collaborated with one of his writing partners, Ken Porter, on a previous book published in August 2012, *German POW Camp 266 – Langdon Hills,* which spent six weeks as the number one best-selling book in Waterstones, Basildon between March and April 2013.

Steve and Ken collaborated on a further four books in the *Towns & Cities in the Great War* series by Pen and Sword. Stephen has also written other titles in the same series of books, and in February 2017 his book, *The Surrender of Singapore – Three Years of Hell 1942-45,* was published. This was followed in March 2018 by *Against All Odds: Walter Tull the Black Lieutenant,* and in January 2019, *A History of the Royal Hospital Chelsea – 1682-2017 – The Warriors' Repose*, which he wrote with his wife, Tanya. They have also written two other books together.

Stephen has also co-written three crime thrillers which were published between 2010 and 2012, which centre round a fictional detective named Terry Danvers.

When not writing, Tanya and Stephen enjoy the simplicity of walking their three German shepherd dogs early each morning, at a time when most sensible people are still fast asleep in their beds.

Index

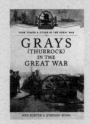

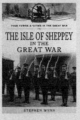

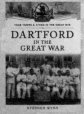

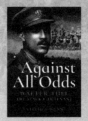